Million Dollar Lips

On the Cover:

How did *Million Dollar Lips* author Joni Rogers-Kante achieve the glamorous look for her photo on the front cover of this book? SeneGence products Joni is wearing include:

SeneDerm:

SeneDerm Dry SkinCare & Advance Anti Aging System
Foundation – MakeSense Advanced Anti-Aging Foundation Beige Chiffon
Highlighter – EyeLuminator

SenseCosmetics:

Blush – BlushSense Red Cherry
Eye Liner – LashExtend Brown
Eye Shadow – ShadowSense – Denim
Eye Lashes – LashSense Black
Brows – BrowSense Light / LashSense Brown
Lip Liner – LinerSense Neutral
Lip Color – LipSense Pink Champagne
Gloss – LipSense Glossy Gloss

www.senegence.com

Cover hair styling by Bridgette Klemect

Million Dollar Lips

A Journey Into the Hearts of Women in Business.

BY JONI ROGERS-KANTE

Foreward by Anthony Robbins

Jerni Publishing
9211 Irvine Boulevard
Irvine, California 92618

Cover Design: Tina Do
Interior Design and Layout: Kiyomi Kajiyama
Copy Editing: Michael Roney, Michelle Gibellino

Printed in the United States of America
Special Limited First Edition (second printing)
Cataloging data and permissions pending

Rogers-Kante, Joni
Million Dollar Lips: A Journey Into the Hearts of Women in Business. /
Joni Rogers-Kante
ISBN 978-0-615-46483-1 (pbk.)

This book is dedicated to You.

Contents

Foreward

There is a process to achieve what you really want in life. Living a life of your dreams requires clarity about what you want, tools and strategies to get you there and personal alignment in your emotions, desires and beliefs.

For many, that clarity, strength and alignment comes only through years and years of hard work and, if you will, personal reprogramming in the quest for fulfillment. Often, the desire to change comes only after many years of confusion and frustration. Too many of us spend too many years not knowing where we want to go.

In other words, we're looking east and watching for a beautiful sunset. What will it take for each of us to simply turn around and see the glorious view?

Joni Rogers-Kante, on the other hand, was blessed very early in life with a series of remarkable and powerful encounters with a Higher Intelligence that brought clarity and alignment at an early age. She then studied under a legendary woman who pioneered a new path for the direct-selling industry, emerging with a clearer vision than ever of her own company, SeneGence, based on a few simple principles.

The principles: Products that really work. A business opportunity for every woman who really wants it. Living life in abundance and love and being willing to work for it. These are the simple yet powerful ideas Joni has brought to the marketplace based on her early life experiences with an all-powerful Creator.

Joni has dedicated her life to molding and coaching women in the direct sales world, much as I have dedicated my energies to bettering the lives of the millions of people around the world through education, training, and coaching that helps others find their true destinies.

Million Dollar Lips is a testimonial to Joni's journey as a businesswoman who built a company of her dreams with others and with a strong sense of destiny. This book serves as a practical guide to help others succeed in direct sales using a nonsensical style based upon truth. She makes it evident that we all make choices in life and business and those choices determine all that we achieve.

Read this book, and you will come away determined to make meaning of your life as Joni has of hers. Whether that guiding voice comes as a thunderclap of our Creator (as it did for Joni) or a child's whisper, you will be determined to listen more closely and put divine guidance into action in your business and personal affairs.

This book will help you discover the clarity, strength and integrity that will enable you, like Joni, to live an extraordinary life.

— **Anthony Robbins**, Author, Life Coach, Entrepreneur

Preface

Though I have written much of my personal history in this book, "Million Dollar Lips" is first of all a book about SeneGence, the company that I founded in 1999.

For those readers who are already SeneGence Independent Distributors, I hope this book will provide you with the framework for an extraordinary career – one that will exceed your imagination while keeping your personal and professional priorities in balance. Wherever I could, I have offered personally tested tips on selling, on building a "downline," on product demos, organizing your home and on many other areas of direct-selling women's beauty products.

Since I expect that many, if not most, of my readers are SeneGence Independent Distributors, I also have tried to remind you of the unique nature of being associated with this company, including your instant membership in the sisterhood of SeneGence Independent Distributors around the world. I hope this book helps spread our sisterhood and encourages women to build upon the truth in improving all aspects of their lives and careers.

If you're not a SeneGence Independent Distributor but are considering a career in direct sales, I hope this book will introduce you to the key concepts that will ensure your success, and also introduce you to the best career opportunity for women in direct sales: SeneGence (Okay, I admit I'm biased).

Even if you are neither a current SeneGence Independent Distributor, nor considering a career in this exciting business, perhaps this book will serve as an introduction to the general world of women's beauty products, direct selling and building a business.

I knew from the beginning of my career that I wanted to capture what I have been blessed to learn and put it in a book that would outline the key experiences, principles and ideas that have led to the establishment of this company. Most of all I wanted to tell the story of how God has intervened throughout my life to help guide me along the way. In fact, there have been times when only God could carry me through the days, and periods of time when his clear instructions were my sole motivation for getting up in the morning and moving forward.

Today, SeneGence is not only a multi-million dollar business enterprise, but it is also an expression of that voice which made itself heard by a little girl nearly half a century ago, laying out a life of servitude and courage to empower others to succeed. For this I thank God for giving me the strength, courage and wisdom needed to fulfill his divine plan for this humble servant while present on Earth.

Though our company headquarters are in Irvine, California, my heart is often still back in Sapulpa, Oklahoma, where I spent my early years of life and learned so much that I try to practice every day even today. Those voices that presented themselves to me as a little girl have helped steer me mostly in the right direction when I have been faced with choices in life and in business. And it is my fervent hope that this book will help other women realize the importance of the choices they make in their lives and careers.

I have been involved in selling women's cosmetics and beauty products for almost my entire adult life, starting with seven years at Sav-On Drugs. It was only natural that I moved on in the early 1980s to Mary Kay Cosmetics, where I rose through the ranks as a distributor until I was serving others in that organization as a Sales Director.

Falling in love with direct selling, realizing it was the perfect way to teach women to build a business, I wanted still more (and had a higher authority to report to) and set out on my own to build a company from scratch. I have seen the direct selling of women's cosmetics from the "Stratosphere" view at Mary Kay and from the ground looking up as I started building SeneGence by personally selling lip color at trade shows. I personally sponsored and trained the initial sales force responsible for the primary growth and success of the company.

Building SeneGence has been my privilege and passion for more than 10 years now, and it has been a remarkable, sometimes tumultuous, mostly joyous journey. I was determined to build a company that offered the best compensation plan in the industry. I also was determined to offer products that unquestionably really work, and a focus on providing every customer with a clear choice of becoming either a retail customer or a SeneGence Independent Distributor herself. In this I, and the multitude of talented individuals who joined in this effort, have succeeded.

Along the way, I also strived to build a company with a culture committed to ensuring success for all women, and a culture that encouraged women to bind together in their endeavor. Our "SeneSister" culture at SeneGence today is unlike that anywhere else. When you are in a room with SeneGence Independent Distributors, you can feel their solidarity and love, their commitment to and admiration for one another and to the company.

I believe God orchestrates the gathering of people to certain ends; in this case the successful creation of SeneGence and to further educate and guide me in the ways of life, love and business.

A few special thanks are in order. First of all, to my mother and father, for supporting me for so many years, even when it wasn't clear if I was going to be able to actually make a living. I hope they can see finally that I have, at last, "a paying job" so they do not have to worry about how I am going to help support my family.

Thank you to Sam and Jennifer Park, who inspired me as their global art business succeeded, and they helped me care for my son Alan when I was struggling as a single mother. Also, thank you always and forever to Carmen Holladay, the consummate giver who took care of me and my son during those early years when I was flying around the country meeting with investment bankers and trying to learn what I didn't know.

This business has taken a tremendous amount of effort from incredibly dedicated and honorable people. To name a few: Michael Moad, our president and Chief Legal Officer, who campaigns for our causes and makes sure we walk the straight and narrow in all matters; Linda Bailey, our first employee and now the "Judge and Jury" of Distributor compliance; Melida Altman, our "Mistress of Money"; Sopath Puth, the "King of Pretty" in the warehouse. To all of these loyal employees, "thank you" is not enough.

And thanks to Cindy, Judy, Marilyn and Kristen, my special girlfriends who have stayed close and nourished me in good times and tough times.

I will always be grateful to Tony Robbins who, from age 22, has been a huge source of inspiration, pushing me to stretch my capabilities and demanding that I "step up" despite the challenges. It has been Tony to whom I have turned throughout the years, in person at his events; on tape and even on television. I see him as he is: much more than a motivator. Tony is a thoroughly modern man who has built a successful business and acumen upon sound truths one can apply to all aspects of life. He teaches spirituality and love as it applies to business.

To Mary Kay Ash I am grateful for creating an entire culture change, and showing women a way to be financially successful at a time when there weren't nearly as many options available for them, and for leading the way in proving that intelligent business women can indeed be feminine, pretty and graceful while building their businesses. I am privileged to pass on many of her sound and kind business practices to the next generation of women.

My gratitude also goes to Neal Offen, president of The Direct Selling Association (DSA), for support and guidance as SeneGence grew. Over the years Neal has led the DSA into a prominent political role and DSA has become an ardent advocacy group for the interestes of direct-selling professionals around the world. He has also frequently inspired me with his approachable style of strong leadership

To my handsome son, Alan, thank you for gracing my life with your presence. You know this journey is and always was in part yours. I pray each night thanking Him for you, his most blessed gift to me. "Be well, my son."

I remain in awe of yet another gift: my husband Ben. Ben is my Adonis. He brings fun, laughter, adventure, elegance and sheer pleasure to life each and every day. I thank you Ben for your strength, prudence, wisdom and unwavering faith in me as we work, play and love one another within this blessed life we lead. Thank you for our little angel, William, who has brought the joys of hugs, kisses, tickles, daily new discoveries and the marvels of mud, shaky dogs and bugs back into focus where they belong.

Finally, special thanks to Christina Aguilera, who uses our products and lets others know how great these products perform.

And thank you to the innumerable women's talk-show hosts, professional career women, starlets, executives, doctors, businesswomen, housewives, politicians, lawyers, and other women from all walks of life who have reignited their own natural beauty with our long-lasting skin-care and color cosmetics.

This book is a testimonial to all of us.

Introduction

Writing the opening chapters of this book, I had the opportunity to recall how "extraordinary" my early childhood was. Heavenly voices have played a lead role for me since age four, beginning with a near-death experience involving a little girl (me) on a bicycle with training wheels, a large pickup truck and a kind "passer-by" who carried me back to my parents' arms.

In this book I have set out to share much of what that pivotal event and a few other encounters with my Heavenly Father have meant as I journeyed along life's course and developed the business and the life of my dreams. Yet, this is not a book about dreams. It is a book about guidance and courage and truth and how heavenly voices have freely mingled with those of my earthly parents and mentors to steer my ship according to a benevolent star.

We all have the ability to hear our heavenly voices, especially as children, if we listen carefully. I was blessed in that I never stopped listening to mine as I learned early on the voice was real and was that of the "Man in Charge" of me.

My childhood near Tulsa, Oklahoma, was painted with the hues of the wind and wide blue skies, and an abundant natural world filled with thunderstorms, tarantulas, breezy meadows and loving parents. I was blessed with close friends and an even closer relationship with God as I learned great life lessons. My basic values were formed early: Fear not, prepare, tell nothing but the truth, find the beauty within everyone and help others.

Later, as I worked through a career at Sav-On Drugs and Mary Kay Cosmetics before starting the company of my dreams, SeneGence, I continued to acquire business acumen and I think surprised many with the enthusiasm and earnestness with which I embraced the business world.

I have tried to share in this book some of the wisdom and encouragement I encountered in my early life and career. Voices of my parents and grandparents, as well as guiding lights in business such as Mary Kay Ash, Napoleon Hill and Tony Robbins have helped me continuously. They opened the doors; We continue walking on together.

But beyond my personal story, I set out in this book to also share some hard-earned secrets and "not-so-secrets" of success in business, particularly for those in the direct-selling industry. Much of what is set out in the book is insider knowledge: direct-selling books are typically heavy on motivation but light on specifics about how to sell, how to build a "downline" and how to run an independent business.

If this is your interest, I think you will find the specifics you seek within these pages.

Do you want to know how much you should expect to earn in direct sales? How many hours a week to spend doing what? How to conduct a Glamour Demonstration? How to sponsor new distributors to your organization? There are plenty of tips and truths for you here.

However, I hope this book serves as much more than a "how-to" primer for direct-selling success. The story of SeneGence is the story of a unique sisterhood of women who have built a multi-million dollar company by sharing in a commitment to serving others and empowering their sisters to be beautiful on every level – to feel like a million bucks! This is what "Million-Dollar Lips" means.

By the time the SeneGence story is completely told decades or centuries in the future, our "million-dollar lips" will represent something greater than the wealth and freedom we already enjoy as the blessings of this company. There is a bond and a synergy that has grown among the women of SeneGence, a commitment to supporting and nurturing each other that is greater than the sum of the parts of our company.

It is embodied in the unique sisterhood of SeneGence Independent Distributors who become organized, efficient, well-put-together women who manage with love. We call ourselves mother, wife, adventurer, priestess, playmate, mistress or businesswoman, and we look good while doing it. We are "SeneSisters."

Anyone who has spent time at one of our meetings or get-togethers knows there is something special in the aura of a group of SeneGence women. It's a spiritual bond. You can join us and find it too.

The concluding chapters of this book provided an opportunity to ponder the future of SeneGence and the future of direct selling. To say I am optimistic would be an understatement. As long as women seek freedom, opportunity, dignity, inner and outer beauty, and the company of each other in a sisterhood of support, there will be a need for companies like SeneGence.

Technology will expand and further contribute to the future of direct selling, as social media and other new channels of communication provide ever-greater opportunities for women to connect and embrace. The face-to-face character of direct selling will endure and become even more cherished. Meanwhile, electronic communications will continue to tear down the barriers between women of all cultures, economies and ages and increase our opportunities to make new friends.

I have faith there is a beautiful future ahead for all women. With this modest book, I hope to encourage you along the path, whether you journey with us at SeneGence or wherever else your heart and your Higher Power lead you.

Along the way, may your life be blessed by meeting many SeneSisters, and may your future be enhanced and sealed with the kiss of Million-Dollar Lips.

Abundance

For attractive lips
Speak words of kindness.

For lovely eyes,
Seek out the good in people.

For a slim figure
Share your food with the hungry.

For beautiful hair,
Let a child run his/her fingers through it once a day.

For poise,
Walk with the knowledge that you never walk alone.

People, even more than things, have to be
Restored, renewed, revered, reclaimed and redeemed.
Never throw anyone out.

Remember, if you ever need a helping hand
You will find one at the end of each of your arms.

— SAM LEVENSON, often cited by Audrey Hepburn

Part One:

Beginnings

Chapter 1
Early Childhood Conversations with God (and Others)

I always tried to instill in all my girls, whether it was in their personal or their professional lives, that they always needed to keep time-tested, high standards in everything they did. Joni seemed to get that right away, and to take it to heart. Even as a teenager, she showed a natural aptitude for business and a profound interest in it, and she started pursuing it when she was just fifteen years old. I used to take her along whenever we'd set up a new store or a new sales market, and she always showed a fascination with the retail aspects of the business.

— JERRY HIGHT, Joni's Stepfather and SeneGence Board Member

My hometown of Sapulpa, Oklahoma, made national news in 2008 when the local newspaper, reporting on the previous night's presidential elections, neglected to mention the winning candidate by name. About the only other time that tiny Sapulpa got that much attention was just before I was born, when two of its younger citizens, known as "The Collins Kids," made the charts with their best seller, "The Beetle Bug Bop."

Sapulpa is a quaint old town on what used to be Route 66. It has a picturesque downtown that looks like "Main Street" in the movies when it's supposed to show how America used to look. Sapulpa is just far enough away from Tulsa to be a small town even today.

I like Sapulpa a lot. It's still "home" to me even though I haven't lived there in decades. I still have dear friends and family there and it's where I learned many of the most important lessons of my life ("Go Oklahoma Girls!").

One of those lessons came on a sticky summer day in 1962 when, as a little girl of four, I was riding my training-wheeled bicycle with reckless abandon, with no sense of limitation, and without the slightest thought of a world beyond my front yard. The cicadas were screeching as they do at midday, and the cosmos was calling me to play.

I hadn't yet learned there are boundaries in life. The world was my playground. So, I ignored my mother's warning about going out of the yard, and went pedaling off into the paved street as if it were another part of an undiscovered continent.

I did so with no sense of danger and no awareness that monstrous things such as trucks are even a part of this world. And even if they are, they certainly posed no danger to me!

My spirited pedaling took me down the driveway and unaware into the sudden roar of a "dragon," when an explosion propelled me virtually out of my body and certainly out of this world. I was hit by an old pickup truck roaring past my home.

To say that I had died at that point is a matter of perspective. Call it "floating." Call it "watching yourself from outside your own body." Call it what you like, but it was "Heaven" to me. There was a bright white light we hear about. More than that, a sense of euphoria overcame me so entirely that I never wanted to leave it. But, as I was enveloped in a sense of love and warmth, a loving voice told me in that instant that I had to return; that it was not my time yet to be in that place of white light, yellow warmth and infinite peace.

At that tender age, and immersed in what can only be described as unconditional love, I felt an energy that clearly indicated I was home and blissfully peaceful. When I heard that heavenly voice, I understood at that moment that my true father was in that "Heaven," and that my own parents in quaint Sapulpa were but my earthly, loving hosts. I was also told in that moment by the heavenly voice that I was put on Earth to do something specific with my life.

I was directed to observe life as it unfolds and to watch and learn and apply what I was to learn. I was instructed to "not be afraid, as I will be with you."

He continued: "You must return to your mother, for it is not your time to be here yet. You have much to learn and much work yet to do."

"No," I said. "I want to stay here with you."

He replied: "You must go to your mother. You see, she is crying."

And I saw that she was.

I was thus catapulted into a life of spiritual, at an age when most girls would have been more concerned with playing house and collecting dolls and watching mother cook.

This may sound like a great deal of responsibility to hand off to a little girl of four. But think about it for a moment. Who among us wouldn't trade everything for that kind of leg up on destiny? Talk about job security! I not only had loving, supportive parents but also a God who had already bothered to get in touch with me ... and to do so personally.

By all accounts the incident was a hit and run. Either the truck that struck me didn't see me or simply didn't stop. I was found on the side of the road by a kind, older African-American gentleman who was wearing tattered overalls splattered with paint. He immediately picked me up from the pavement and walked with me cradled in his arms, from the road up to my front door. I observed this from above.

This mysterious gentleman had witnessed what had happened to me and related the sequence of events to my astonished and frightened parents. It was as if he appeared out of nowhere, performed this spontaneous act of kindness without seeking reward, and then disappeared.

He left me in the safe care of my mother and father and walked away from our home, never to be seen by me or by my parents again.

When the truck hit me, I flew over the bicycle's handlebars and was heading straight for the curb. The impact was painless and instantaneous. My wondrous journey thus began.

My wounds were minimal and not serious. I recovered quickly and painlessly.

Of course, as this four-year-old girl began to tell her story of floating with angels to a loving place of white light and complete peace, the adults around me were glad to see me recover but dismissed my recounting of a spiritual inner experience. Their skeptical compassion was as accommodating as that of loving parents and friends could be of a four-year-old girl's apparent fantasies, especially as I recounted that I watched the scene unfold as if I were looking from the upper corner of my living room, watching my mother sob over my body lying still on the couch.

And yet it also became obvious to everyone, my mother and father included, that I had undergone some sort of transformation in and through that accident. My behavior immediately became that of a girl much older than me. My interests shifted, as did the entire emphasis of my life. I was no longer the typical little girl fixated on the entertainments of childhood. Humanity and the ebb and flow of energy, and its cause and reaction, began to fascinate me. The world of adults — their language, their perspectives — seemed more intriguing to me. Some children naturally gravitate toward adulthood. I didn't. I switched into "adult" life in that instant.

My newfound affinity for grown-up living seemed to be the direct result of my death and life experience and the understanding that there was a Heavenly Father (known to me as "God") who guided everything I did. Whatever the reason, it was the beginning of a whole new level of participation and purpose in life. I became absolutely fearless and I embarked on a life fully fascinated with all that unfolded before me on a daily basis. At four, my life was gifted, purposeful and directed. I began to plan not to waste a single day of blessings.

During my early childhood, so many of my happiest moments were spent on my paternal grandparents' nearby family farm, where I lived with my dad, William (Bill), and my older brother Billy (My mother and two younger sisters had already moved to California to begin a new life).

There is something about a farm that can be magical, especially for children. The closeness to Nature and the "circle of life" experienced first-hand through animals and plant life is something that lives on within a your consciousness for an entire life span, even if you leave the farm.

4

I was on our farm when I learned one of my life's most valuable lessons, this time from Grandpa Lenial Rogers himself.

Like it is yesterday, I still remember the day Grandpa Rogers entertained us in the barn with a giant tarantula that he found nearby.

Tarantulas are, at best, fearsome, furry, creepy animals, filled with venom and put on Earth for the sole purpose of killing other creatures. At least, that's what I thought when I was seven. But that day in the barn I learned that fear is relative to the potential for harm and I learned that fear is mostly unwarranted, if you are prepared. And once you realize that harm usually comes only to those who are unprepared, life takes on a whole new meaning. This was the day I would learn that we can, by preparation, fend off even the scariest potential predators in our lives.

When we first saw the tarantula crawling on Grandpa Rogers' cracked leather boot, we were terrified, especially when Grandpa let the creature crawl farther up his bootleg. I didn't realize that Grandpa was putting on a little show for us children, to make a point. As the tarantula moved from the tip of his boot up to the ankle, my grandfather pulled his blue jeans tightly to the back of his leg so that the venomous creature had no leverage to crawl up under Grandpa's jeans and make contact with the skin.

"You never need to fear," he said before finally and decisively brushing the tarantula off his leg and out the barn door. "You can protect yourself against anything if you anticipate a problem, understand the potential for harm and know how to prepare to prevent harm from happening."

That lesson had glue. Superglue! It has stuck with me forever, and it helped me prepare for or eliminate many potentially difficult life challenges and gave me confidence I could learn how to deal with new situations over and over again. In that moment I was reminded to never fear, always prepare, anticipate, be willing to do the work and trust the voice inside my head. Most of all it taught me that when a situation seems ominous, there's always a solution —

you simply need to seek the answer.

Often, answers come to me in life through the voice of my Heavenly Father. And one of my most memorable farm experiences as a little girl was another "conversation"with Him. There is a vibrant life-energy that you find in every corner of the farm, an energy that is spiritual. Everything is blossoming, growing, nourishing. There is a spirit moving life all around you, in you and with you. You can feel it in the wind.

I have read scientific explanations about why Oklahoma is so windy, but I don't really understand them. I do know that parts of Oklahoma are often continuously breezy, including Sepulpa, and the wind is enchanting. As a result, the scent of grassland and barns and fertilizers and life travels far and wide. The "circle of life" is evident and abundant.

It isn't surprising then, that my next heavenly encounter, three years after the first, occurred amid the natural setting at the farm. This time my heavenly voice was instructing me on another vital aspect of living.

On the periphery of the farm there was a large rock formation that overlooked an incredibly beautiful meadow of native Indian Grass and wheat grown for hay – tan and green and supple as it waved and crooked in every breeze. I would go to that meadow in my private moments, to commune with nature and to gaze upon the shiny lake that sparkled like a diamond tiara in the late afternoon sun. Mostly I would retreat to my lovely reddish sandstone hideaway to pray and to have those private conversations that little girls of seven have with their dreams and with God.

That private retreat was also a place for reflection and thanksgiving. And late one afternoon when the sun was getting low to the west over the nearby town of Stillwater, and the trees and brush around me cast magical golden shadows, I felt the glorious presence of God once more.

This day He was telling me that I had a big job to do, that my life would be unusual and exceptional ... and He reminded me to never be afraid. When a doorway to a new opportunity was presented to me, I was to walk through it, just as I was to recognize each experience as a preparation for the next. Big words for a small girl, but I understood. I understood then that I had a lot of work to do. His voice told me that when I couldn't walk the path myself, He would carry me. I would never be alone. Whatever I was to do would reach around the globe and affect millions of lives.

Since that day, I have made it a life's habit to pray for courage, wisdom and strength of heart and mind to see me through the mission I was given by my Creator. Even today. I teach my sons to pray in the same way.

Throughout my life, I have been fortunate enough to have prayers answered, in fact and directly. And isn't the realization of one's prayers the ultimate affirmation of faith? At this point, let me qualify the fact that I've had other visitations from Him (I think we all do) but this moment at my sandstone retreat was one of the most profound and abrupt interventions from "angels," guiding me from harm's way.

Imagined? Inspiration? I know what happened. I can say in truth it doesn't matter how these happenings in my life are perceived. I know they occurred, and the fact that they did enabled me to get through life, with all its challenges and opportunities, with a continuous sense of trust accompanied by such an overwhelming feeling of gratitude that I simply could not fail.

Yes, I've been blessed. Looking back, one of the greatest blessings bestowed upon me was the understanding that I was always to listen to my "inner voice." I recognize this voice as the voice of my God. His voice has been my guide always.

There have been times in my life when I have not listened closely to this inner voice, and the choices I've made in those moments have not been positive.

As life becomes busier — with energies being expelled in so many directions as businesswoman, wife, mother, sister, daughter and friend — my challenge and my prayers are geared toward being more aware and listening to my inner voice, the voice of God, which I believe are, most of the time, one in the same.

Philosopher Dorthea Brande once said, "Act as though it were impossible to fail." Imagine if you were able to conduct your life that way. What great things could you accomplish?

We are all the sum of our experiences. That's what makes us unique. The issue on this journey of life is what we do with the experiences we have.

Let me tell you one last story from my early childhood, an event that taught me one more valuable lesson.

Children can be tactless at times, more often than not without meaning to be so. That was the case with me when, as a small girl, I pointed my finger at an obviously disfigured old man whom I happened to come across in a store. He was wrinkled, old, hunched-over with a noticeable hump on his back that some older people get. What's more, he looked sour and, to my tiny child's mind, without redeeming qualities.

My dad, William Rogers, was standing next to me. Dad was a big man, six feet and four inches tall. He was rugged, charming, handsome. Dad loved people and people loved him. He was a true tough guy, a U.S. Marines veteran of the War in Korea, but he had the heart of a kitten.

At that moment dad sensed my reaction and took me aside immediately. He assured me that this very gnarled and seemingly unattractive old man had remarkable qualities, that weren't visible to me – qualities he challenged me to see by looking more deeply, beyond the obvious.

Dad urged me to understand that inside this man, whoever he was and whatever his circumstances, was here for a reason; a reason apparent to and designed by God.

In that moment, in the corner of that general store in that small town in Oklahoma, my dad's words sang a chorus of truth and a deeper way of seeing. If nothing else, this man I happened upon in that store was here to give me a gift of humility. In that moment, I fell in love with all of humanity.

Since that day, I regard everyone as equal and equally valuable in their own way, regardless of stature, race or background, knowing that our Father in Heaven loves each of us, as He had shown me through and through to my very core. There could be no greater gift to a small girl than that kind of insight, and a wave of respect naturally began to flow from it. That moment, that confrontation and the lesson that came out of it, changed me forever ... and very much for the better.

I've learned to always keep an eye out for the true gift in life: people. I learned to look into others' eyes and see their special gifts, beyond physical appearance, clothing and accessories. I believe God has a purpose for every encounter. I strive to become a gift to others with each meeting. I look for the uniqueness of every human being.

There were other lessons I learned as a child on the Rogers' farm.

I learned the importance of personal pride and the fundamentals of beauty from my Grandmother Rogers. Despite her age, she was the most beautiful woman I knew.

Fastidious by nature, she was a model of both efficiency and decorum. Even though she lived on a farm and rarely entertained outside company, she gave tremendous priority to looking her best at all times. From the moment she awakened in the morning she was busy washing shampooing, curling her hair, putting on her makeup and donning her nicest clothes, sewed by her, always cleaned and pressed.

Her reasoning was as infallible as it was simple: "It's important to look your best for the people you love most," she said. And what could make more sense than that? If charity begins at home, so does consideration.

Up until that point, I had never even thought about my personal appearance and grooming, or anyone else's, as being of any importance at all. Now, here was my grandmother — someone I both loved and admired — giving such tangible emphasis to what most of us take for granted. I was fascinated watching her apply makeup each morning. She stood in front of the small bathroom mirror holding a thin black Viviane

Woodard lacquered compact containing what seemed like an endless selection of gorgeous shades of powder. I was riveted as I watched her apply various powders to her face, cheeks and eyelids with brushes of all sizes.

Everyday she was a new masterpiece. I saw this ritual as a work of love in motion. I was inspired. She demonstrated that personal grooming and appearance is a proclamation of respect for others as well as for you.

Fast forward 35 years: My husband Ben and I were shopping for manufacturers that we might consider for acquisition to shore up the SeneGence supply chain and avoid future mishaps. As we were walking through the floor of one of these companies, I stopped dead in my tracks as we passed by a showcase displaying one of the black makeup cases I had seen in the hands of my grandmother so many years ago.

Our host noticed my reaction to the product and guided us into a section of the building where women gathered for makeup instruction. I was standing in the very room where Vivian Woodard taught her "beauty consultants" make-up and selling techniques!

I burst into tears as overwhelming feelings of love and a memory full of joy of my living grandmother surged through my body and mind in that moment. I turned my head to Heaven and cried prayers of thanksgiving and gratitude to God as I realized I'd come full circle; from a life's inspiration to my destiny.

One of the benefits of finding a sense of direction early on was the fact that I was able to go to the "school of life" with some very bright people — many of them in my own family. My sisters and I not only had exceptional grandparents, but also two sets of very bright loving and devoted parents. And I have always felt that I have had not one, but two terrific fathers.

My Stepfather, Jerry Hight, ("Dad Jerry") is not only a great dad, but also one of the most astute businessmen I ever met, and I credit him for so much of the marketing and personal management acumen I have learned over the years. I know him only as "Dad," or "Dad Jerry," and I say that with the love and affection of a doting daughter. And he, in

turn, refers to me as "daughter" with a reciprocating love and respect.
Even at 15 years of age, I was fortunate enough to be allowed into his world, and to see first-hand the best aspects of logic, reasoning, loyalty and leadership. He was Senior Vice President of Merchandising at Sav-On Drugs, so he knew the privileges of upper management, as well as the responsibilities that came along with them. At that tender time in my teenage years I was a sponge for information, as you can well imagine. I wanted to learn everything! And with Dad Jerry's help I learned many, many good business practices.

One of the early lessons I learned from him was the importance of business ethics — to take the high road and, when in doubt, to grant others their own level of both trust and dignity.

Dad Jerry emphasizes the importance of taking time to think things through. He is a firm believer in the retail philosophy that "the customer is always right," and that doing the "right thing," whether it be easy or difficult, is the only way to operate.

He also instilled in me the simple belief in the old chestnut of wisdom that there are no free lunches. In his words," The harder you work, the more substantial your reward. True ambition always stands out as long as it comes with a set of high standards and strong personal ethics." I learned from him that you do indeed reap what you sow.

I guess it's not surprising then that even now I go to this man as a consultant when some important decisions are to be made with my business. He provides balance, perspective and surprising objectivity.

Dad Jerry also clarified early for me the importance of "Defining Moments," which I discuss often in this book. Dad taught me that defining moments can happen in an instant or over a period of time, but they always alter our lives in irrevocable ways.

One such defining moment that Dad helped put in focus came in the late 1970s, while I was working on a Grand Opening set-up crew for Sav-On Drugs.

The first day I walked into a newly constructed but empty building,

I felt a lump in my throat as I wondered how we could ever install display fixtures, check and price merchandise, stock the entire store and train a crew in time for the planned Grand Opening. Accomplishing such a daunting task required me to rise to a level of performance I previously thought impossible. Those pressure-packed days taught me how to perform under pressure, how to work on a team, how to understand the range of possible outcomes and analyze a situation, and how to jump in and get a job done.

Dad taught me that "we become what we think about," and to accomplish the seeming impossible requires focusing on positive outcomes and applying oneself 100 percent to the task at hand, maintaining consistency and dedication.

In that defining moment, I learned by watching my Dad and learning how to lead through kindness, direction and expectation.

Dad taught me these critical lessons about life and business:

1. **Brainstorming is Powerful:** Gathering many peoples' ideas, comments and possible solutions often leads to easier and more productive ways to attain goals, solve problems, and tackle challenges. No one person has all the right answers. It is critical that every person who is in any way connected to the goal, problem, or challenge being addressed be brought into the brainstorming discussions and takes part in defining solutions and strategies. It takes a team, and the cooperative intentions of each team member.

2. **Routine Standard Operating Procedures:** Standard Operating Procedures, or business rules, save significant time and increase productivity and efficiency. Creating documented standard operating procedures that are shared and practiced among key team members and associates saves time and money because "the wheel does not have to be reinvented continuously." Hence suggestions on how to divide time,

increase efficiencies, and delegate productive activities are mentioned throughout this book.

3. Communication is more than just saying or writing words. The light bulb must come on in the minds of both the communicator and the person who is receiving the communication. If this does not occur, the intended communication has not been achieved. Watching the eyes of the person receiving the communication will often signal whether the light bulb came on or not. That's another reason this business of direct sales and one-on-one relationship building works so well – often the most productive sales, training, and sponsoring events happen "eyeball to eyeball."

4. Take good care of your horses. Some members of the original key management team of Sav-On Drugs were of the Mormon faith with backgrounds in agriculture and farming. They understood very well that the *work gets accomplished* by "the horses" and *the horses need to be well taken care of* to ensure that the work gets done. At SeneGence that translates into providing the best of the best for each distributor who does the work – the best products; the greatest opportunity to earn the highest returns for sales income and commission income in the industry, sponsoring bonuses, car programs, rewards and prizes, exotic trips and lots of fun!

5. Efficiency and productivity generally peak when the workload seems "undoable." Human nature is such that the time required to accomplish a job expands with the time allowed. The great majority of people perform at their best when their workload seems almost impossible. The busiest people are the most productive and get the most done. Choose to work with busy, productive individuals. The seemingly undoable will be achieved.

6. Project set-up time is significant. Project set-up time is important and needs to be properly controlled. Planning and preparation is a very important function needed to achieve goals. Pack your own parachute. Prepare to win. The set-up work needs to be accomplished in advance of scheduled appointments so others are not standing around and losing interest while waiting for the set-up work to be completed. Idle time is wasted time for the bottom line and end result!

7. 1+1 = 3. That's synergy. When 1+1 equals 3 (or possibly more), synergy has occurred. Synergy means the working together of two (or more) things to produce an effect greater than the sum of their individual effects. In SeneGence there is great synergy whenever you mix phenomenal products with a fantastic compensation opportunity program and the efforts of amazing achievers:

> Products that Really Work
> + Career that Really Works
> + You & Me
> _____
> SeneGence Success!

≈ Your Turn (Chapter 1) ≈

I invite you to take a measure, or inventory, of the life-changing experiences in your own life. Use the following worksheet to spend time reflecting on your early life. And take note of the handful of life-changing experiences that affected you from that day forward.

1. List any miracles that might have taken place in your life. We've all had them. The key is in recognizing them. Don't be shy. And don't limit your perceptions. George Bernard Shaw wrote that, "Life itself is the miracle of miracles." Start there and the rest will fall into place.

2. Think of three experiences you had as a child that might have altered the course of your life or your attitude towards your future. How did you respond to them? Did you learn from them? And did you put them to use? *(Hint: They don't necessarily have to be bolts from the blue, divine white light or some kind of epiphany. We can learn from adversity as well.)*

3. Think of at least three people who have been the most profound influence upon you in your life. *Hint: They may or may not be from your immediate realm of experience. They could be anyone. They can be people you've had interactions with at any level — spiritual, personal, business, sports, travel or social activities.* They don't even have to be positive influences (though I hope they were). Let's just say that the encounters and associations made an impact that stuck with you. If so, how did they stick and

Your Turn (Chapter 1 cont'd)

what kind of impact did they make? How did they influence you and why? And did you put it to use? Does it serve you or is it best to now eliminate that belief?

4. **What use of these people, places and opportunities have you made today?** Are they still a part of your life? And how have you changed because of them? Did they empower you? Or weaken you? (And were you able to recognize it?) We are only as effective in our lives as the use we make of our experiences. Nothing can be more self-defeating in life than to experience a crowning achievement or a bleak, abysmal failure (And we've all had them!) and bring nothing from them. The successes and failures you've had are gifts in your life. They're there to be cherished, learned from and made use of in future dealings. That's exactly why you were given the chance to experience the event or situation! Grow from it!

Chapter 2
Teachers Who Show the Way

When I began my SeneGence journey in 2005 and made my first trip to California to meet Joni at Seminar, I had no idea how life changing that trip would be. I remember introducing myself to her and her telling me she too was an Oklahoma girl, so we immediately had a bond. From that moment on Joni invested herself in my business and in a personal relationship with me. There was a time when Joni and I spent weeks on the phone together going through Napoleon Hill's book, *Think and Grow Rich*. She showed up even when it was just me left on the call and I knew she had plenty of things she could be doing! She sacrificed her time to help me grow my business and grow as a person. I could go on and on about this woman and how grateful I am to her, and how blessed I am to be part of such a special company. We have fantastic products, but really we share much more, we are a family.

— DAWN CHRISTIAN, SeneGence Independent Distributor (Royal)

In addition to the many things I learned about life and business from my family, I have been blessed with other mentors who have helped guide my path.

I believe mentoring is responsible for 90 percent of human development. It's the way we align ourselves with our daily behavior. And in turn we are constantly mentoring others, through our words and our actions. Most of us don't realize how significant our words and actions are on the thoughts and behavior of others.

Every day I choose which of my mentors I can turn to for guidance, depending on the situation I am facing. Often, I begin by choosing to emulate the thinking of Jesus Christ. I ask myself, as the bumper sticker suggests, "What would Jesus do?" I have found this especially helpful when the question I am facing is at a high level.

In business situations, I often model my decisions and actions on what I think Lee Iacocca, the former CEO of Chrysler (and, before that, president at Ford Motor Company) would do in a similar situation. Iacocca is not only well-known as a business leader, he is also known for his courage and vision.

We have to be careful picking mentors, because our choices will determine if we are functioning at a higher level than simply wandering willy nilly through life.

I've met many of my mentors through books. I read as much as I can. I've read hundreds of business books, self-help books and other publications about how to live and love.

However, learning from other business leaders can only take you so far. You can internalize information from books but you must take it further, and learn to imagine the conversations that you would have with a particular writer or teacher or mentor. I use these great teachers and my imaginary conversations with them as a starting point for my own thinking about a particular problem.

Mary Kay Ash, the founder of Mary Kay Cosmetics, used to say, "Hitch your wagon to a star." I try to do exactly that, but sometimes even today I find myself wondering what it means. I *think* it means you don't just "hitch your wagon" to anybody. You have to be careful whom you emulate.

You certainly don't want to hitch your wagon to people who are negative, people who are not achieving positive growth in their lives. Negativity breeds like mold, gradually creeping into places where you can't even see it and making everybody around sicker and sicker.

It's also important to learn how to listen carefully. I strive to be an expert listener. But it is equally essential to always think for yourself, evaluating what you hear and picking and choosing the ideas that are helpful to you. I like receiving advice but rarely follow it "to the letter," because I know opinions are just opinions, even when they come from the wise.

Of course, mentoring is more than sharing opinions; it's showing others a way of life. And actions speak louder than words, so to be a mentor you've got to walk your talk. You've also got to be willing to step out and walk your own path, not just follow exactly in someone else's footsteps. You think for yourself.

Even as a young girl I was aware of the difference between my thinking and that of others. I learned to appreciate that difference and to learn from people without giving myself away to others' prejudices or shortsightedness. I learned to "take the best and leave the rest." So I'm a firm believer in always maintaining a healthy skepticism. I apply that healthy skepticism to just about anything anyone says.

The teachers I had as a young girl at Washington Elementary School in Sepulpa were among those who helped me develop my independent thinking even at an early age. I always looked at teachers with great reverence, knowing that they were highly educated. I value knowledge so I value teachers.

My favorite elementary school teacher was Mrs. Hansen, who was large, very German and strict. I respected her because she didn't let me get away with stuff like others did. Mrs. Hansen was tough. If I forgot my homework I would go up to her and give her a smile and tell her a cute little story. I would be thinking, "If I'm cute, she will just pat me on the head, and let me get away with not having my homework."

But instead Mrs. Hansen would look at me unflinchingly and say "Okay, Joni, you forgot your homework, that's an 'F.'" She didn't buy into my excuses.

I liked her because she did not make a distinction between whom she favored or didn't favor based upon charms or looks. She demanded results. She treated everyone the same – with equality, strength and kindness in the classroom.

I learned to appreciate and admire those who treat all with fairness and kind even-handedness. To me, treating everyone fairly and evenly is a sign of respect to all individuals who are, for whatever reason, gathered together for a common cause – whether it's work, church, home or wherever.

My best friend in school in Sapulpa was Kristin Zumwalt. Kristin's mom and dad were and are today wonderful people. He's an accomplished doctor, and she is a powerful Republican Party advocate in the state of Oklahoma.

They lived in a beautiful home only a few blocks from the modest house where my family resided. My family actually lived in a series of homes, though, moving often when we could not keep up with expenses. Kristin's family, on the other hand, was well-to-do, and their home was lavishly appointed.

I spent most of my free time at the Zumwalt home, where I was always generously welcomed.

Being in that home helped develop my political views, which are exactly the same as Kristin's parents – traditional, conservative, valuing initiative and self-reliance.

The Zumwalt home was my safe haven. The family took me on vacations with them, and they treated me like a daughter. I ate many, many meals with them. They are a very kind and giving family.

The Zumwalts showed me what was possible in life. They showed me that it was possible to be kind and loving and have an organized, healthy family life. They are just as strong and loving today as they were back then.

The other lesson the Zumwalts taught me is the importance of practicing random acts of kindness and influencing others to do the same. I go into more detail about that a little later in this book.

I recently talked to Kristin on the phone and asked about her parents. As it happened, her mom and dad were there with her in the car and they were all on the way to the wedding of a family friend. The Zumwalts – still together as a family after all these years.

Alas, all good things eventually come to an end and as much as I loved the Zumwalts and the other wonderful teachers I had in Sapulpa, I physically left that world behind me when I moved to California at age

15 to live with my mother JoAnn and my new dad, Jerry Hight.

I left because I was instructed to, following my involvement in a highly unlikely and bizarre "incident" in which my good friend Jeff was accidentally shot in the rear – by me!

Jeff and I were best of friends. We were two of a large circle of good friends who gathered for parties and events throughout the school years and summer breaks.

One beautiful Oklahoma afternoon Jeff and I went target shooting under the bridge near our neighborhood. It was a typical country scene: a couple of kids with feet dangling over a river, beneath the railroad tracks, whiling away the time, target shooting. At one point I set my pistol down at my side on the old wooden bridge and it accidentally fired a round. It shot him right in the butt.

He wasn't hurt too badly, but it was still a traumatic incident because just two weeks earlier one of our friends was shot and killed by accident.

That afternoon we both heard the gun go off, of course. Jeff and I immediately looked at each other, because neither one of us had a gun in our hand. We both stood up, and we looked at the guns on the ground, and they were still lying where we set them. Then we checked each other and that's how we found a hole in his trousers where he was shot!

Well, in the aftermath it seemed like everyone was wondering, "What kind of girl would be out shooting a gun anyway?" Jeff was in the hospital, I was in tears, and Mrs. Zumwalt took me to her home. She intuitively knew I would need the loving arms of a mother that night. Kristin and I snuggled into a warm bed and talked all night. I cried more, Jeff got better, there were no hard feelings and I even wore his bracelet after that.

But now a familiar Heavenly voice, the same one that came to me earlier in my childhood as I described in the previous chapter, came to me again. This time it said, "You have learned all you can here. It is now time to leave. There is still much to learn."

Meanwhile, Dad Bill determined that I had served my time in Sapulpa. He said I needed my mother … and college opportunities that were hard to come by in Sapulpa. God's guidance gave me the courage to uproot my life and start anew with a family I hardly knew. So when it came time for my first year of high school in Sapulpa it was agreed I would move to Southern California to live with my mom and Jerry Hight (whom I came to call "Dad Jerry").

Oh my, what a change it would be. Now I would begin making the transition into adult life.

During the next couple of years, while I was living with my mother and Dad Jerry, I developed a better-than-average work ethic. But you wouldn't have known it from my high school grades. I was a very good student in Oklahoma, but started struggling in high school in Ventura, California.

I found myself in a terrible, shy stage as I began attending classes at Buena High School (home of the Bulldogs!) in Ventura, near the foothills of the Los Padres National Forest and just a few miles from the beach.

In this beautiful setting I went from being a yearbook queen in Oklahoma to being someone who could only look at the sidewalk while walking from class to class. I couldn't even answer teachers' questions, although I desperately wanted to. I was learning how painful it is to be shy. That's one of the reasons I feel so blessed today to have a company that makes products dedicated to helping women feel more confident about themselves.

My best – and *only* – friend at Buena High was Sandy. She was in the homecoming Queen's Court and was a cheerleader. I was blessed to have her in my life and she helped me get connected.

Meanwhile Dad Jerry, a Sav-On Drugs executive, helped me obtain a part-time job at the local Sav-On Drugs store, though I didn't talk much more at work than I did at school. But I sure could listen and take instructions and do what my Dad told me. He looked at me during that time and saw someone who was eager to work and learn.

At the time my life seemed to be headed backwards. The only reason I stayed in California was because I had been told by my Heavenly Father to "step through every door." What I now know is that at that time I was being taught humility in a big way.

Anyway, I worked my way throughout high school and, after graduation, found myself with a new business mentor: Mary Kay Ash, the founder of Mary Kay Cosmetics.

I became a consultant with her company because I wanted to go into business for myself in my chosen field – cosmetics and personal care.

Sav-On Drugs, meanwhile, was going through corporate downsizing and centralization, becoming streamlined and centralized to the point that every store looked the same. Previously, every store had been run as a separate business, which was the big appeal for me. With that business model soon to end, I realized it was time to move on.

I also realized at Sav-On I could not make the same business decisions those men who were running the stores were making – at least not in an objective manner. I was more emotional than they were, and in particular there as no way on earth that I could make the decisions they made regarding employees. These were hard decisions affecting the livelihoods of many people. I still can't do that today.

So, I told Dad Jerry I wanted to work with people, but in a different business. After unsuccessful inquiries at a few places, I was introduced to the concept of Mary Kay Cosmetics by my roommate. I became a Mary Kay distributor in 1982, and started learning from Mary Kay immediately, even if it wasn't a one-on-one relationship. She had the ability to make you feel like she knew you personally, even if you only saw her twice a year at management meetings and conventions. She could assess someone very quickly.

At this time I rented a two-bedroom condo in Woodland Hills, California. It was a lovely space surrounded by park-like terrain of running streams and trickling water that reminded me of the farm in Sapulpa.

My roommate was actively selling Mary Kay products. I watched her day after day as she arrived home after conducting presentations, organizing her inventory, counting her earnings, all the while paying her share of the bills on time. Finally I said to her, "Tell me more about how this works," and I went to a meeting with her. The rest is, as they say, "history."

I took my Sav-On work habits with me into my new career, and in two months, working the Mary Kay business part time, I matched my 60-hour-per-week income at Sav-On.

I began learning about Mary Kay's business and life values through her books and through weekly communications. She taught me a lot about positive affirmations.

Instead of the corporate world – where it seemed everyone was looking for their co-workers' flaws and making judgments about what people were not capable of doing – Mary Kay looked for the good in everyone. This resonated with the way I wanted to spend my business efforts – encouraging others to do well.

But Mary Kay could be tough, too. And she made whatever decisions she needed to make based on *truth*, regardless of the popular consensus or just how the numbers "read." This appealed to me from the very beginning, as I knew a true entrepreneur must be able to lead with heart, not just numbers and reporting alone.

Mary Kay was also very involved in politics and used her position to influence others – another thing I liked about her. She had earned for herself a position in which she could speak the truth and people would respect what she had to say, particularly as it applied to politics, and I think that is one of the greatest services you can provide to the community.

Last summer Dorothy Zumwalt recalled for me a story that tied together a "destiny moment," that is, an important moment in time which, recognized or not, sets to pattern for one's future.

One summer in the mid-'80s I planned to drive to Oklahoma for a visit, and Dorothy agreed to host a cosmetic party so I could count the trip expenses as a working event. While there, I convinced Dorothy to become a Mary Kay distributor.

I was thrilled she agreed and continued to call her from time to time to see if there was anything I could do to help her in building her business. Over time, I realized she only became a beauty consultant to make me happy, with no intention to actually sell products (ah, the things we do for love!).

Now, 25 years later, I learned that prior to my arrival in Oklahoma back then, Kristin and Dorothy had just returned from a Republican Party fundraiser at Mary Kay Ash's home in Dallas. Dorothy told me that Mary Kay had suggested to her that she should become a beauty consultant, and then a director for Mary Kay Cosmetics in Oklahoma, as it could give her an influential platform to touch the lives of women throughout the state. Dorothy had gracefully declined Mary Kay's invitation.

As Dorothy shared this story with me, I suddenly realized that I had successfully recruited a woman that Mary Kay Ash herself couldn't recruit! Wow! Mary Kay would have been proud of me. No wonder she once looked directly into my eyes, smiled, and said, "You're one of us, aren't you?" My response: "Yes m'am!"

One day I would like to teach women not only how to run a business from home, but also how to help influence support for our right to life, liberty and the pursuit of happiness in this country. I plan to take a stand and be a voice to secure, for our children in the future, the freedoms we enjoy today. All in due time.

Another important lesson I learned from Mary Kay was how to extend the average day to accomplish more. She was a big believer in waking early, before other people. She taught us to get up and start work early. By doing so you gain an entire workday each week.

I learned to put my best foot forward, regardless of what was happening in my life. I learned to leave the kids and the house at home, and concentrate on showing up for business looking 100 percent professional and efficient, always.

Those lessons remain with me in my life today, maybe more strongly than ever. And I call on them to help guide me in my business life. That was evident recently while I was preparing for our annual SeneGence Seminar, our premiere event for SeneGence Independent Distributors. I write the entire staging script for Seminar every year. I also play the main role as emcee onstage and I am the main trainer. I love doing it. But this was a tough Seminar year for me because my dad was in Arizona going through open-heart surgery. I was torn about where to be. Still, I knew that dad would not want me to shirk my responsibilities. I kept in mind the image of Mary Kay Ash, willing to work as the leader of her company despite the tragedies that happened to her family, in my mind as I worked on.

Although dad's surgery was not a tragedy (he recovered quite well), it was a distraction while I was trying to lead the Seminar. It turned out to be a wonderful event. In fact we set up a computer in the middle of the room, logged onto Skype, and dad joined us for Seminar during his waking moments.

After Seminar, many of the attendees said it was the best one yet! No one knew or suspected the stress I was under. Mission accomplished!

Mary Kay Ash was my first business mentor outside my family, but she certainly wasn't my last. As I mentioned previously, another was Lee Iacocca, the former Ford Motor Company executive who took over as the head of Chrysler in the 1980s.

Iacocca mentored me through his books. Probably the most important value he taught me is not to engage in activities that don't generate replicable income.

Applying his lessons to the direct-selling business, I realized that the two most important activities in direct sales are 1) demo-ing, which generates sales income through reorders, and 2) sponsoring, because that generates ongoing commission income. I'll address these things in more detail in chapters 10 and 12.

According to Iacocca, everything in business is secondary to generating income.

One more important teacher for me has been the 20th Century writer Napoleon Hill. His book, *Think and Grow Rich*, teaches the characteristics you need to be successful.

Hill taught me how to develop internally the skill set that I need to be absolutely successful at whatever I undertake. And you know who told me to read Napoleon Hill? Mary Kay Ash!

Early in my career I wrote Hill's 13 characteristics for success on my bathroom mirror and each morning I would think about the things that I had done yesterday and the things I had to do today, and how I could best apply each of those 13 steps to my actions. And I did it year after year after year.

So books are a great resource for learning and growing. However, nothing takes the place of a living, accessible mentor who effectively helps you unleash your personal power to live fully and to capture your dreams. This is what author and visionary Anthony (Tony) Robbins has helped me understand.

I was first introduced to Tony at a hotel in the Los Angeles area while in my early twenties (As I recall, I paid $15 at the door that day and could not afford to return the next).

I remember this tall man-of-a-man telling the small gathering how he helped a woman overcome her fear of snakes. Through the following years, I had the opportunity to attend Robbins' seminars on personal growth, spirituality and health, both as a guest of others and as a ticketholder. From time to time, I've taken guests of my own to his events as well. I continue working with small groups under Tony's guidance and spending as much time with him as available, treasuring every bit of insight I can receive from this remarkable man.

In my estimation, Tony is something like Napoleon Hill on steroids. Tony takes you through a series of tested and proven processes that physically and emotionally change old realities (perhaps learned through environmental factors such as demographics, religion, country of origin and family traditions) and help you discover if the "old truths" serve you well. Perhaps these "old truths" need to be replaced with new realities (based upon your dreams and desire) that will in turn serve you in achieving your dreams. This is a simplified version of a much more complicated process.

I gain insight from Tony regarding business development, financial management, people management, social contribution and so much more. As Tony and his business and training content continues to grow, so too does my understanding in these areas, and in turn this acts as my inspiration to continue to develop innovative products and processes for the company. Tony is a giver and is kind enough to lead the way for millions of searching individuals around the world like me.

In turn, I like to think I am both a giver and a mentor for the many women who are SeneGence Independent Distributors.

I wish I could be a full-time mentor to many SeneGence Independent Distributors, but my job as CEO of the company requires that I am engaged in different activities. If I ever found a CEO to take my place I would gladly go back out into the field and work directly with our wonderful Distributors, attending to field activities such as demo-ing, sponsoring and training. What a great life career that is – making women feel more confident selling products that really work and teaching those who choose to do the same!

Never be reluctant to look at other industry experts, or other top Distributors, in the party-plan, demo-ing, direct sales business, to be your mentors. Be on the lookout always for new teachers.

One great place to look is at your own upline (for those unfamiliar with direct-sales terminology, this is your sponsor into the business). But ultimately it doesn't matter if that person is not a strong mentor or role model. She can still be your upline, but in that case you will have to look elsewhere for your inspirational role models. Remember: "Hook your wagon to a star."

If you can't get the mentoring you need from your own upline, look online and find someone such as SeneGence Independent Distributor and Queen Jerry Taylor-Swade, who has a great attitude and is always willing to share her experience and strength. Send that strong leader of your choosing an e-mail and tell her you'd like to learn from her. Believe me, if she's the right role model she will be delighted to help.

Successful SeneGence Independent Distributors are eager to mentor others who show the courage and the drive and have a vision to become successful. There's plenty of room at the top.

In the long run, in direct sales it's essential you build relationships and allow yourself to be mentored by those more experienced, and then, in turn when you are ready, you graciously mentor others and build a cycle of success.

The SeneGence Independent Distributor knows that the cycle of training is essential – "SeneSential!" It's a given within our SeneGence culture. Our top "royalty" are taught they will train anyone and everyone in their area, even those not in their "downline."

One last recommendation for finding mentors and generally building your skills and motivation: Attend local events and presentations from top sales motivators and business developers, "how-to" sessions. You can usually discover these events listed in the local newspaper business section or a local business newspaper.

Attending these event helps you fend off others' counterproductive actions and speech patterns that otherwise would undercut your consciousness. They help build your arsenal of information and knowledge to succeed, and help propel you forward toward the achievement of your dreams.

Remember, if you want to be a race horse, learn to run with the race horses. Look for other direct-sales professionals with whom you can become friends and share accountability as you build your career. Everyone should have a library of positive, motivational CDs in their cars. Listen to company and industry-related CDs instead of listening to music channels. You will find you are enjoying hours of training time in your car each and every week.

Gaining inspiration and knowledge from others is simple and oh-so-enjoyable. By listening to the wisdom of others, you'll have more fun, and your business will grow even faster with the right influences impacting your decisions on a daily basis.

❧ Your Turn (Chapter 2) ❧

• Can you name three people in your field or career whom you admire? List them by name, and write down the reason you admire each of them. Determine if you can apply some or all of the traits you find admirable to your own life/behavior/speech.

• If you are a SeneGence Distributor, can you name three other Distributors or SeneGence Leaders who exhibit the qualities you would most like to develop in yourself? What are those qualities?

• Ask yourself this: "What are the qualities I currently need to develop to move forward in my business life?" Name three SeneGence Leaders who exhibit the qualities you would most like to develop in yourself. Assess your opportunities for growth regarding these qualities, and write them down. Can you adapt these qualities so that they serve you well?

• Have you ever had an incident in your life that looked like disaster at the time, but turned out to be a blessing in disguise? I bet you have! Maybe that family relocation that led you to just the right place, or that lost boyfriend you cried over just before you met the Love of Your Life. Spend a few quiet moments in reflection over these hidden blessings, then name them and write it down. Note how they became blessings in your life.

Chapter 3
SeneGence: A Dream and a Way of Life

Joni has always had a completely independent way of operating and functioning. Her thoughts and perspectives are so entirely individual they can only be correctly described as unique. When she commits to something, whether it's her business or her personal relationships, she gives it all she's got.

— MILLIE BREY, Joni's Younger Sister

In my early twenties I decided that college wasn't right for me. Dad Jerry told me that if I wasn't going to finish college I had to figure out how to make it on my own. Becoming an independent distributor for Mary Kay Cosmetics got me started.

I thought being an independent distributor would provide a safe route to becoming a business owner. After all, I figured, the company founder had already done the footwork by putting the corporate infrastructure in place. That meant I did not have to worry about the details of management nor the cost of its overhead; I could focus on building my business.

As great as working with Mary Kay Cosmetics was, I eventually found myself wanting more, especially from the compensation structure. I also envisioned products that were capable of nourishing a woman's skin while making it more beautiful. I wanted color that would not come off when my son, Alan, then an infant, played with my face and innocently smeared my makeup.

I wanted the color to be skin care and the skin care to stay put.

Yes, I wanted it all!

I had the idea to write a business plan for a cosmetics business centered on two very simple ideas: offering women products that really work and offering a career that really works by selling those products. I had my own ideas about what kind of compensation that career should offer, based on how I would like to be compensated for helping to build a brand and what kind of products I would like to represent. But above all, my ideal company had to offer products that worked. There had to be no question about the products. Truth would be built upon truth.

With the encouragement of my friends and family, I energetically moved forward with my business idea. But I had recently become a single mother, and I knew it would be a while until my company could produce any kind of significant income to support my son Alan and me.

It was a difficult, lost, confusing time. In my marriage I had realized that "if you can't fix it, move on." I left my first marriage and my early direct-selling career behind, and I was consumed with formalizing the ideas for SeneGence in an organized manner.

I moved into the home of my dear friend Carmen Holladay, who helped me care for my little son. There I was, completely mesmerized as weeks slipped past while I wrote the business plan for what eventually became SeneGence. Moving in with Carmen, who had also recently become a single mom, was definitely the right decision for us.

I remember Carmen sticking a dish of food in front of my face while I was writing one evening. I was sleeping in front of the computer night after night. With a limited knowledge of computers, I wrote financial projections on sheets of paper, one taped atop another into a roll sometimes 12 feet long to complete a computation.

I thank God for Carmen and for everything she did for me during those tough times. I hope I have paid her back in full and more but will always feel gratitude for the love and support she continues to shower upon me and my family even today (As many of you know, she is still a vital member of the SeneGence organization). Carmen is my son Alan's "second mom" and is "Auntie Carmy" to my little son William.

Looking back, I see now that from the beginning I always was cared for, financially and emotionally, by loving friends and family. Their generosity and support enabled me to take the time to develop this company.

During this period in the mid-'90s, as I was adjusting to life on our own and living with Carmen, I set about finding people to help me develop the products I envisioned, and the structure needed for my company. I knew I wasn't a chief financial officer, so I had to find one. I knew I wasn't a president, so I had to find someone for that role. And I sure knew I wasn't a chemist, so I had to find someone who could help me create the products I described in the business plan.

I spent three years traveling around, learning what I didn't know and looking for people who could help me implement what I was learning I needed to do.

There were some early failures — and I thank God for those! When I look back at those false starts — including incomplete contracts for taking a new and different product line into direct sales using my original concepts and theories — I know there was a familiar hand guiding me along, even though those false starts seemed like setbacks at the time.

Then, in 1998, I ran into a man who knew of a chemist who was working on something that sounded close to what I was looking for as my ideal color product. It took three months just to get a meeting with this well-known product formulator, but I finally had the opportunity to sit in front of him and present my business plan. He had a new product that he allowed me try out on my lips. I thought "Wow, this is really close to what I had imagined!" and I told him so.

That product was a little different from what is SeneGence LipSense today, and it was in a blue and silver shiny tube and named "Ultralux." It contained some of the same ingredients that would eventually wind up in our patented SeneGence product, and it was far better than any other lip color I had seen at that point in my life. I applied the product right there in the chemist's office, and bit at my lips to see if it would smear or rub off. It would not!

He read my business plan and said "Joni, if you can do with my product what you say you can do in this business plan, we've got a deal." We shook hands. We operated as partners on a handshake deal for that first year. Later, he told me he knew I "was the one" when he met me. He meant the one who could take this product, sell it, build a business around it and brand an entire line of products that really work.

I know there are many business people out there who would have called out the lawyers and written up contracts to seal the deal. But that isn't how I think. If I can't do a deal with someone based on a handshake and their word, then I don't want to do it at all. I have learned over the years that a piece of paper means nothing. It's the person you are dealing with that really counts in business. Contracts and legal matters have their place, but they are not the foundation upon which to build long-lasting relationships in life or business.

The chemist's faith in me as "the one" gave me strength to do right with his formulas and forge ahead building this business despite the obstacles and difficulties that bubbled up so frequently in the early days.

✍ Your Turn (Chapter 3) ✍

• Psychologists point out that grateful people are happy people – They have more positive emotions, personal satisfaction, compassion, and less stress and depression. **Take a moment right now to make a "gratitude list" – a brief inventory of the many blessings in your life.** For me, the list would surely include the many people such as Carmen Holladay who took care of me and my son while SeneGence took shape. Another is my son, Alan, who inspires me to be the best I can be. Start your own gratitude list right now, and include at least 10 people, places or things in your life for which you are thankful. Keep your list handy (in a pocketbook or wallet, for example) for those moments when you're feeling down, and update your list at least once a year!

• Can you trust others to keep their word? Do you keep yours? **List three examples of important agreements you have made in life and business that were based on mutual agreement and a handshake.** How did these agreements enhance your life and make you feel about yourself and others? How did they change the course of your life?

Chapter 4
SeneGence: Building a Brand That Really Works!

When I first joined SeneGence as a Distributor I caught the unique power of the products almost immediately. Originally I remember thinking, "Every woman in America is going to want this product." And having a unique product is the foundation of any successful business.

— JERI TAYLOR-SWADE, SeneGence Independent Distributor (Queen) and Washington State Founder

My original business plan for SeneGence envisioned a full range of advanced skin-care products and a completely integrated line of color cosmetics that stayed on until removed and at the same time made skin more beautiful. Happily, that is what we offer today, but for the first few months of our company's history it wasn't quite so.

When I first met with our original chemist in 1998 at his office in Riverside, California, my great idea for a company was based on a business plan that required $3.7 million to get started. My task, after our handshake, was to set out to find the money I needed by talking to investment bankers and venture capitalists all over the country.

I packed my things into a couple of suitcases (honestly, I did my best to pack lightly!) and set off across the country armed only with my business plan, a vision of integrated skin-care and color cosmetics that really work, and a sample of the initial lip product.

I traveled by plane to cities such as New York and Dallas, and by car to San Diego, Los Angeles and elsewhere in search of the capital needed for the launch I envisioned.

In meeting after meeting, those venture capitalists and investment bankers wearing dark suits, white shirts and red ties just looked across their impressive chrome and glass desks and smiled wryly, dismissing my idea as unsubstantiated or unsophisticated.

They didn't know much about cosmetics or skin hydration but they sure knew a lot about what can go wrong with startup companies and they were looking to deal with men in Brooks Brothers suits, not some feisty cosmetics gal with a vision of girl-parties and cosmetics that work. Well, what did they know about products that really work anyway?

There were some long, silent cab rides after a few of those meetings. At times, I wondered if they were right and I was missing some key ingredient needed for success. Maybe I wasn't sophisticated enough to pull it off. That's what they seemed to be saying. Their pessimism was a far cry from the supportive, encouraging words of Dad Jerry or the product formulator and others who kept telling me, "Joni, you've got it right. Now is the moment!"

Plus there was an even higher Heavenly voice, one I met as a four-year-old girl in that not-so-accidental meeting with a truck in front of my home, that kept telling me to walk on, walk on. It reminded me that this was what I was meant to be doing.

I walked away from meeting after meeting frustrated but not discouraged. Meanwhile, I was learning that I would have to start up my dream company more slowly than I originally planned, using cash from sales to fund growth.

In April 1999 I first started selling a lip-color product known as "Ultralux" to raise the initial investment cash. These start-up months gave me time to hire packaging designers for my own products and to work with the chemist to develop the formula for LipSense.

During that time we set up a "warehouse" in Newport Beach, California, in a mobile home I shared with my son. The living room became our warehouse, the dining room became the clerical office, and my bedroom served as the computer room and order-entry department.

Alan and I had moved to that neighborhood as a result of a suggestion from dear friends Sam and Jennifer Park, who also lived there. Sam and Jennifer were busy building their names as world-class, museum-grade artists, and we were able to share childcare responsibilities. When they traveled, their son stayed with me, and when I traveled Alan was with them. This park had a gated entry and was near their school – Newport Elementary. And, let's face it: The rent was affordable.

A year later, in April 2000, SeneGence was able to move into its first headquarters in a real building, a warehouse and showroom in Newport Beach. We had space, but no furniture. So my good friend and benefactor Carmen Holladay and I drove up to the warehouse district in Los Angeles and purchased office furniture and decorations for our new corporate offices. I think we did a darn good job – we still use that furniture today. In fact, it still looks as good as it did in the beginning.

Ben Kante, later to become my husband, joined the SeneGence staff that spring, and in April we held our first Seminar in the parking lot of company headquarters for 65 of our enthusiastic Distributors.

Those early offices had enough office furniture for most of us. Ben, however, had to sit on the floor for his first days with the company. We were trying to keep up with our growth as best we could.

Ben had joined the company to spearhead our communications and media team. It was love at first sight – that is, for Ben and Alan. They instantly bonded. Ben, already well traveled and a world explorer, has since taken Alan to no less than two countries per year as part of Alan's education. They have seen the world together as they learn about cultures from around the globe. Alan continues to travel to new countries every year, completely on his own or with friends. He has remarkable instincts. Knowing this and observing his trust in Ben, I decided I should take a closer look at this Gentle Ben too.

At the same time, we began discussing a possible exploratory trip to Vanuatu, a cluster of small islands in the South Pacific, to gather raw materials for our skin-care line.

Our chemist had introduced me to a recognized botanist who studied primitive plant sources that could be used for skin-care products. The botanist told us that the plants and minerals near the base of the giant and active Yasur Volcano in Vanuatu contained natural ingredients that were potent with curative and protective properties not available anywhere else in the world.

We all agreed that Vanuatu sounded like a perfect living laboratory for the collection of new natural ingredients that could make SeneGence skin-care products more effective than anything ever seen before.

And so in the fall of 2000 about a dozen of us, including Ben heading up a team of photographers and videographers, boarded a plane in Los Angeles and set off across the Pacific Ocean for tiny Vanuatu in search of a better way to protect and enhance the natural beauty of women's skin.

By jet, small plane, boat and truck we trekked to our lodging close to Yasur, and camped in exotic (read, "primitive") quarters nestled among the lush tropical vegetation and native tribal people of Vanuatu. The botanist and the chemist led the group on expeditions into the rainforests and along the base of the ashen volcano itself, collecting and labeling samples of rocks and ash and plants that were then carefully packed and shipped back to California for laboratory testing.

Those dozens of cloth sacks of samples yielded revolutionary results, and laboratory tests in the U.S. confirmed, to my joy, that our suspicions were right. The natural chemistry of the fertile soil near the base of the Yasur Volcano and the rich coves of the South Pacific were producing raw ingredients that could be assimilated into SeneGence products with unprecedented protection and support – qualities that would change the nature of women's cosmetics and establish a much deeper meaning to skin beauty.

Immediately after the trip and the lab tests, we set about incorporating these ingredients into our proprietary SenePlex Complex formulation that is the base of the SeneGence SeneDerm Skin-Care and SenseCosmetics product line.

Less than two years after I first presented my business plan to the chemist, we were actively developing and selling our own revolutionary products based on science and natural ingredients. We were accomplishing what the venture capitalists in New York, L.A., San Diego and Chicago said was impossible.

We had gone from selling Ultralux at trade shows such as the Chicago Home and Garden Show to building a million-dollar company with products that work based on our own research and ingredients and marketing ideas. Meanwhile, our Independent Distributors were prospering through our unparalleled compensation plan.

In our first seven months we sold $1.7 million in products at shows and conventions. By the end of our first year we had more than a thousand Independent Distributors. In the next year our sales hit $3.8 million. We were well on our way to success.

Though many Independent Distributors in those early days were still selling LipSense and our first skin-care products at trade shows, others were beginning to realize that the real opportunity resided in sponsoring other Independent Distributors at home demos and building their own Independent Distributor sales forces.

Meanwhile, Ben, my future husband, became the "jack of all trades" in our early company. In addition to heading up our media department, Ben began the work to standardize the designs of the SeneGence brand, logos and trademarks. These are things I would never have thought of. Ben also understood the complexities of international business development, setting up a global money-transfer system that enabled us to recruit Independent Distributors in other countries besides the United States with the same level of compensation enjoyed right here.

Ben, along with Michael Moad, our company president and legal guru, also helped me sort out which products to incorporate and which to eventually abandon. Michael has been a guiding force at SeneGence since those very first days and has always added a level of discipline and good sense that has enabled us to survive and prosper. What would I have done without him during that tumultuous time?

Both Ben and Michael are examples of how a businesswoman can succeed by surrounding herself with talents other than those she was given by her Maker. By surrounding myself with these two men, I have been able to focus on marketing SeneGence SenseCosmetics™ and SeneDerm® Skincare products while they have steered the business on a successful course through the perilous high seas of growth.

One product that unfortunately never succeeded for SeneGence was our original line of nutritional supplements. Our vitamin line featured an oxygen-infused formulation developed for us by the renowned Dr. Kurt Donsbach, a well-known pioneer of alternative health. Dr. Donsbach and I are believers in the importance of good nutrition and abundant oxygen to support deep beauty and skin care.

I still believe that our work with Dr. Donsbach was another demonstration of our commitment to a product line that really works for women. At SeneGence, our view of cosmetic beauty goes well beyond surface appearances. But that's another conversation to be held at a later date; one we will have in the future and that will play into our unwavering commitment to building a brand that really works.

⁓ Your Turn (Chapter 4) ⁓

• Sometimes, surprising ingredients are the key to successful products. Did you know that Worcestershire sauce gets much of its unique flavor from anchovies? Who would have thought orchids, which SeneGence incorporates into our SenePlex formulation, are a key to long-lasting skin care? **Can you think of other examples of situations that 'came together beautifully,' and consisted of a surprising mix of people and coincidental incidents that made a dramatic impact in your life?**

• **Make a list of your five top talents in business.** Don't be shy; Give yourself credit where credit is due. Write down how you use those talents to be of benefit to yourself, your family, and others around you. Now list your five weakest areas. Be tough; make sure you name five of them. Now, for each of your five areas of weakness, name somebody in your personal or professional life who has a special strength in that area. See how this works? We give, where we can, to the benefit of ourselves and others while at the same time we surround ourselves with people who balance us, who have God-given talents we lack. Think about how you can learn from these people around us, and how you can surround yourself with their talents.

Chapter 5
SeneGence: A Way of Life

There are so many aspects to this company and so many opportunities for growth that sometimes it's overwhelming. I've had opportunities to travel and broaden my horizons. This career I've taken on has improved my confidence — about myself, supporting others, and gaining lifelong friendships. It's all a part of a greater dynamic. I feel like I'm a valued part of this family, and I feel like I'm building my own general family around me. Making money is a blessing of course. But the most important thing to me is the success, happiness and sense of fulfillment of my downline. It means so much to me – even more than my own success.

— SHEILA YOUNG, SeneGence Independent Distributor (Crown Princess)

From the beginning I envisioned SeneGence much as it is today: a party plan, direct-selling company. Our primary sales channel would be individual Independent Distributors selling our products at small gatherings – mostly at friends' homes and offices. Advertising would be largely through word of mouth, and we would build credibility through "wowing" women: demonstrating our products in person to one or several women at a time.

But we didn't start out that way, because initially we did not have the money to put all the party-plan products and tools in place. We had remarkable skin-care products and complementary-color cosmetics, but we didn't have product samples, demo kits, follow-up brochures and other essential marketing materials. In those first months and years, we couldn't afford those things.

So we did what we had to do to get the company going: We traveled to conventions and trade shows and just started selling products. And we were selling as quickly as we could get products out of the boxes and on display. In fact, at most events, security guards were posted near our booths to keep the aisles clear enough to control crowding. Our demos were continually active, often with 10 or more women deep around each demo table.

Though our trade-show sales were generating cash and bolstering our confidence, we were still only reaching a limited number of women and constraining our growth opportunities.

I could see trouble ahead for our sales model: There was such strong desire for these products that Independent Distributors could make a lot of cash just selling at trade shows.

My plan was for SeneGence to be a lot more than just a snappy-selling trade show product. I wanted to change women's lives with a great product and a great, mature business plan that touched women's lives around the world. I wanted my Distributors to find a career in direct sales, not just a quick buck. I soon realized I would have to lead the way and begin showing Distributors the payoff that results from sponsoring others in a sustainable manner and obtaining commissions from residual "downline" sales that paid well into the future.

Still, it took a great deal of effort and, eventually, unity to convince that first wave of SeneGence Independent Distributors that trade shows were not best for the business; that we were intended to be a party plan direct-selling company. We lost many of those early Distributors as we eventually evolved and fulfilled a business model that provides for longevity and prosperity for all who "do the work" in direct sales.

By 2003, to help turn the tide in the right direction, I began a new training process: conducting "road shows," traveling and personally teaching Distributors how to conduct in-home product demonstrations ("demos"). Some pioneer Distributors embraced that concept and stayed on. Others were only interested in a quick sale at a trade show, which meant very little follow up and follow through for their customers, and no ongoing support for those they sponsored at the shows.

I knew then, as I know now, that follow-up with customers and support for downline Distributors is a must. It is impossible to teach women at a trade show everything they need to know about developing beautiful skin through using these marvelous products, or about running a successful home-based business.

Resolving this issue was a matter of business survival. It was a difficult transition, but we had to do it in order to fulfill our mission and to be a company that would last for generations. I learned how difficult it can be to truly tell the truth, no matter what.

I am so grateful I had the support of my husband, Ben, who encouraged me to forge ahead as planned, and to evolve our business from tradeshows to home and office demos. Today our Distributors are much more prosperous, running businesses with very low overhead, and spending time home each and every day with their families instead of traveling to trade shows and conventions. In fact, some are downright "celebrities" in their own communities, often called "The Lip Lady," in their social circles.

Of course, their success is also a result of selling great products. We do not launch a product unless it really works. It must truly produce results and meet the claims we make about it. We don't just rely on marketing, we rely on science. We do not put into place a Distributor support program or process unless we know it to be of real benefit to our customers.

That's why I say that if a woman wants to run a business out of her home, SeneGence is the best opportunity there is. SeneGence has the absolute best compensation plan found in the direct-selling industry, though I'm not sure our Distributors always understand that. But it's true! The SeneGence compensation plan provides the financial payout I would want if I were the person continually selling products and developing downlines.

Unlike other direct-selling companies, SeneGence doesn't engage in what is called "breakage" – reducing your commissions on sales by your "downline" – the women whom you sponsored into the business

– as you or they become more successful. And that makes us the most profitable company a Distributor can represent. Generally, as a result of "breakage," you lose the commissions you were previously earning as that person and their downline organization "break away." After one of your downline Distributors is "broken away" you receive only a fraction of the percentages you previously earned for that "leg" of your organization. This makes no sense to me at all! As a Distributor I want to continue to receive full commissions on the entire organization I bring into the business, especially if my organization is successful. So at SeneGence, regardless of how successful a Distributor in your downline becomes, you will always continue to earn the same percentage level of commissions that you earned on downline sales from the very start.

Another reason SeneGence is absolutely the best opportunity out there is that it's easy to represent a product line that really works. With such great products, you don't have to learn fancy, challenging sales techniques. Our products are "Wow" products, and when women try them, they actually say "Wow!"

A SeneGence Independent Distributor buys her inventory at up to a 55 percent discount off suggested retail price. We have one of the highest sales-earning opportunities in the business. For instance, if you sell a product for $100 (U.S.), you can make $55 (U.S.) on that $100 sale. Now that's girl-size earnings!

I say "girl-size" because SeneGence is definitely a company for women. We don't have many men actively selling products in our sales force. Instead there are a lot of women who, like me, would prefer to work with other women.

What a blessing it is as a woman to be involved in such a big way in the cosmetics industry. Women love cosmetics. It's an industry for women. We know what we want! We have fun with it. So our work is our fun. In fact, when I'm traveling people sometimes ask me if I'm traveling for work or for pleasure. My response: "My work is my pleasure!"

Working in a woman-based organization, SeneGence women tend

to be closer to one another than they would be at companies where there is a broader mix of men and women. At this company, we hug. We get to know each other's kids. And we get to know what happened to the baby, or to the father, or the grandparents of the woman standing next to us. We have those conversations when we see each other at trainings and Seminar and elsewhere. We care about each other.

That's what SeneGence Field Leader Distributors like Sheila Young and Cathy Hoolihan are referring to when they talk about the "sisterhood" of our Distributors. It's a "SeneSisterhood" of women. When you work and play in a caring and nurturing culture, it's extremely comforting to realize you have a sisterhood of friends and associates whom you can count on.

Often someone who is not yet a SeneGence Independent Distributor but has just experienced us as a group at Seminar, or on a Webinar, or even during a phone conference, will comment on the strong bond between SeneGence "sisters," a bond they can hear and feel – even over the phone! I love those comments. It makes me proud to know that the SeneGence Sisterhood is a safe haven and a place of love, fun and caring for those who care to partake.

SeneGence offers its Distributors the opportunity to be successful entrepreneurs, with the same business opportunity that I have minus the corporate overhead and its challenges. We all sell the same products, but Distributors don't have the challenges and time-demands of running the infrastructure of a company: The IT department needs help as new viruses are bombarding the system; the new packaging was destroyed in shipment; the Marketing department needs more information from me to meet a deadline; our scientist is working on a new product. These are the issues I deal with every day so Independent Distributors can focus on selling and building a business of their own.

SeneSisters agree there is a SeneGence way of life. It's about waking up with or without an alarm clock, spending time with your child or your loved ones in your home in the morning, getting the morning started off on the right foot: hugs, kisses, seeing everyone off to where they're going. It's about spending your time at work involved in activities that generate income. You get to the office by 10. Your work time is spent wowing, booking, demo-ing and directing customers or Distributors, doing beneficial and productive money-producing work during the short time that you are away from home.

At the end of your work day, around 4 or 5 p.m., you go home to enjoy a lovely evening with your family.

You can earn ample income for vacations, college, a new home or redecorating and even a car (that SeneGence will pay for, if you do the work). Even if you are a single mother, it is all there for you.

To me, that is living the dream, all the while building, over time, a substantial business you can leave to your children.

Every thing you do as a SeneGence Independent Distributor is about working for yourself and your family.

I hope you've already joined us, or you will soon. Maybe after reading this book. Rest assured your efforts will be generously rewarded with an enriching experience, building a business with a brand of products that really work.

⤠ Your Turn (Chapter 5) ⤠

- There was a song by Lovin' Spoonful that asked,
"Did you ever have to finally decide?
Say yes to one and let the other one ride?
There's so many changes and tears you must hide.
Did you ever have to finally decide?"

Has this ever happened to you in *your* life – reaching a point where you were faced with choosing which of two roads to take, knowing that one keeps you in your current "comfort zone" while the other leads to an unknown future and greater risk but also greater reward? If so, how did it turn out? Did you make up your mind to "pick up on one and let the other one ride?" Are you willing to make tough decisions now for the betterment of the future, even when they hurt?

- **What does a "dream job" look like to you?** Do you prefer a structured day, waking up on time, getting to work on schedule, getting home according to the clock? Or do you prefer to mix your workday with family commitments and caring for others? Do you prefer working mostly with women, or do you want to work with mostly men? What monetary goals are important to you? Vacations? College for kids? A new home or car? Do you believe you can have it the way you want it? Take a moment to write down what it is 'exactly' that you want. Commit to yourself a plan that includes a way to learn how to get what you want.

Part Two:

Lessons

Chapter 6
Building on Basic Values: Truth

Joni's given me the gift of self-confidence and unlimited possibilities. After more than 20 years in the military as a leader, I had no clue what I was going to do when I retired, and honestly, the SeneGence opportunity basically saved my life. Joni's beautiful spirit, her love, generosity and passion show me that if I walk and work in truth, if I'm dedicated to my goals and never give up, I can do and be anything!

—KELLY ROBERTSON, SeneGence Independent Distributor (Royal) and California State Leader

I believe the most important value in any business is a commitment to living in the truth. Companies, like individuals, should maintain an overriding commitment to integrity, honesty and plain, simple truth. That is certainly the case at SeneGence, and it is an important part of my business plan.

If you make a business decision based on anything other than the truth, you are wasting your time, energy and money. A decision based on anything other than the truth will not last. Stick with the truth, no matter what.

That's how we approach single decision we make at SeneGence, and that's how I approach every decision in my life.

If you know me, you know *that's* the truth.

When I make a decision, I first ask myself, "What would Jesus do?" I know you've heard that before. But I really do try to remember to first pose that question every time I make a decision.

Next, I consider whether I am basing my decision on sound and truthful analysis. I visualize my mentors, I imagine which one is best suited to make this particular kind of decision and then I ask myself what decision that person would make if faced with the information and circumstances I am facing.

I've learned the hard way that a decision is only as good as the information upon which it is based. Learn to check the facts.

Napoleon Hill's book *Think and Grow Rich* makes a strong case for the Biblical principle that nothing stands without truth. This is more than theology — it is, in fact, a surefire way to make good decisions in business and in life.

Because I am an emotional creature, I had a tendency in the past to make decisions based on whether I liked someone. Too often, those decisions came back to bite me. I've learned that making a decision based on compassion (a true virtue in its own right), instead of truth, gets you in trouble. If you focus on the wrong motivation, you make the wrong decision, and you make it for the wrong reason — it's skewed by falseness.

Some years ago we had two high-ranking executives who tried to convince me to "borrow" some computer software without paying for it. Those execs were tip-toeing around the truth, asking my permission to steal, to use software the company hadn't paid for. It set off all kinds of alarms for me. When someone wants to initiate a business practice based on lying or cheating, how can you trust that person? Needless to say, those two executives are gone from SeneGence.

This commitment to truth also applies to how I sell, and how SeneGence Independent Distributors are expected to sell. Don't lie. You don't need to lie. Great products "wow 'em" on their own!

The same applies to flattery. I don't flatter people unless I mean it. It's straightforward: If you don't mean it, don't say it. Remember what my mother taught me (and maybe your mother taught you too!): "If you don't have anything nice to say about someone, don't say anything at all."

For SeneGence Distributors conducting Glamour demos, I urge you to just be yourself. Be who you are and be honest and you'll get further — people will know you are being genuine. Again, it's easy when you have products that work. Simply "show and tell" the product and your guests will be wowed. No need for flattery at all.

Our top royalty — the highest-ranked Distributors in SeneGence — *have* to be an honest group of women because you can't have a long-lasting following of customers without being truthful.

In the past, some direct-selling companies engaged heavily in misleading representations of products and opportunities, but that's not the case anymore. The tide has changed – people today don't fall for fake sincerity, or for false advertising – they want to buy from companies and Distributors who can give them good counsel and products that really work.

At SeneGence, product claims are based upon clinical trials. So we can demonstrate that our products actually work. And our compensation program works, too. That's the plain truth.

The truth is a high standard, and I think it's a high standard that other successful businesses adhere to. Most successful companies are committed to telling the truth, delivering an honest value/service/product, or they don't stick around long enough to talk about it.

Building on falsehood is like cutting corners while building the structure of a large high-rise office building. You leave out this brace or that support and eventually, without that support, the building crumbles.

I don't believe a company can last 50 or 60 or 100 years unless there is first some kind of honest, no-corners-cut, solid working structure supporting it.

Think of other companies in our industry that have been around for a long time. At the core of most of these companies are the values of the people who began the business. These companies were built on solid business practices and structures at the beginning, and that's why those companies are still around today.

Choose to build your business on solid ground, using tried and proven practices such as the SeneGence Independent Distributor training programs, and your business will flourish and sustain you for years to come.

There's more to business than making money. It's nice to be able to pay bills, but I rarely consider the bottom line or long-term impact on potential sales increases when an individual is trying to encourage me to make a decision that just isn't right for our culture. As I said earlier, I lost a couple of good executives over their inability to base decisions on long-term sustainability and security in lieu of short-term gain at the cost of truth.

Another SeneGence value is faith. One of the proudest moments in my entire career was when a speaker at our annual SeneGence Seminar remarked, "SeneGence is obviously a Christian-based organization."

Her remark was directed to the entire audience, hundreds of SeneGence Independent Distributors gathered at that event. I was sitting in the back row of the auditorium taking notes on my laptop, which I always do. When she made that remark, tears welled in my eyes (Okay, by now you've probably guessed I cry a lot – it's true). I looked at my executives seated on either side of me, and they didn't seem surprised in the least. Wow! Another destiny moment (see Page 23)!

I felt the love and warmth flowing around the room that day as never before. And I remembered the words spoken by Him in my childhood: " … and what you build will be felt around the world."

When I heard that Seminar speaker make the comment about our company, I was shocked, thrilled and humbled because, as a rule, at SeneGence we do not put into print anyone's religious beliefs or teachings – not in our literature, marketing or presentations.

So this particular speaker was making that comment based on our actions and the emotions and feelings she gathered from her brief visit with us. Now that's something to be proud of.

Another important value at SeneGence is the sanctity of the family. I make family a priority everyday, and I think every woman should. That's why we are in this business, isn't it? We want to be loving, fulfilled women at home, and have a positive effect on the emotions and lifestyles of our families, of those we love.

Having a good work ethic is yet another value we treasure at SeneGence. I say, "Choose to live life in love and abundance, and then work for it." That means you have a role, a choice, in what the results of your efforts will be. But you have to choose abundance and then be willing to work for that. It also means doing the "right" work so you are not wasting your precious days.

In order to live a life of abundance you have to plan for balance in your life. I talk a lot about this in trainings at various levels in our company. You have to plan for work time and for family time. You have to learn how to compartmentalize, so you can show up and be 100 percent engaged in whatever it is you're doing at the moment, within whatever schedule you've designed.

In other words, when you spend time with your family, just spend time with your family. I've even stopped bringing my laptop home from work in the evenings, because I've realized that when I have my laptop at home it infringes on my time to spend with my little son William. What kind of balance is that?

So you have to schedule time for family – and that means time with your spouse as well.

Ben and I make Friday nights "date night." Although we work and live together, we often don't see much of each other as a result of our busy schedules. It's comforting to know that at the end of each week we will come together simply as a couple and enjoy one another's company.

On Friday afternoon I have lunch with my son Alan to ensure we stay connected and I am in touch with his development, interests and pursuits.

We schedule Sunday night dinners for the whole family. It may be a yummy meal at home or we go out to a favorite Japanese restaurant we've been eating at since Alan was 12 years old: Kitayama in Newport Beach. We make sure we are there on time and "show up" for each other.

And every morning when my little one wakes up, that morning time is my very own time with him. We play games, sing songs, snuggle and tickle, make breakfast. And yes, now we get him dressed for school. How time flies!

That's where getting organized and planning comes in. It starts at home with your loved ones.

Getting organized is a learned skill. You're not born that way, you have to learn how to organize yourself, your clothing, your home, your family time, your work time, social time, spiritual time, education time, financial planning time and stay-in-good-health time. Without good health, great quality time spent in other areas becomes more challenging, so be sure to plan time for getting and staying healthy.

I did not use a date book until I learned how to use it as a tool to be more effective, more efficient and more organized. Now it's the main tool for organizing every area of my life, including family and business and all the other categories I mentioned in the last paragraph.

Every personality type can and must learn how to plan well if they choose to live life in love and abundance.

Remember, you reap what you sow. If you're very unorganized, you can't sow much, because you're drowning in clutter.

When you visit my house and open any cabinet or any drawer, you will find complete organization. It saves time and money. It helps eliminate replacement costs of missing items and the time spent looking for items not put back where they belong.

This topic is so important I dedicated Chapter 21 of this book to "Getting Organized at Home."

Another important value in our business is continuing education. It's a challenge for me to find enough time to continue my own education, but I know I need to always keep trying to find the time to learn more. For this I've committed daily time between 4 p.m. and 5 p.m. that I devote to my online education. I also keep a rotating stack of books at my bedside to read before sleep instead of watching TV.

Finally, the successful businesswoman has to put a high value on cultivating the quality of faith in herself and, in the long run, the big picture that what we value will come to be. You have to be able to move forward without always knowing all the facts of a particular situation. Picture the end result as it applies to the area of interest – family gatherings, business acumen, friendships, spirituality, etc. What does it look like? Feel like? What is your perfect moment for it – whatever you are doing and what moments are happening that signify you are living your dream at the moment?

Define these things; Be clear and precise. Then begin the journey to success by putting one foot in front of the other and have faith that you will discover all that you need while walking down the path of your destiny.

You will gain confidence and faith that as long as you are making decisions based on truth you will successfully propel yourself forward.

Move forward with truth. Just move in faith. That's the key.

I know you can. And remember what He told me: "I will be with you."

❧ Your Turn (Chapter 6) ❧

• How important do you think it is to tell the truth? **Can you think of past and recent instances when you have compromised the truth in order to avoid some imagined negative response from somebody?** Do you remember a time in your life when you told a lie and it turned sour? Maybe when the truth finally came out it made matters worse? Or someone was hurt by your lie? Can you commit to a life aimed at "truth"?

• Although SeneGence is not a religious organization, "faith" plays a key role in forming our values, and our distributors and customers can hopefully see that. **Can you name two other companies that represent a value-based business culture?** Think for a moment ... do you prefer doing business with companies that "stand for something?" Or do you make purchasing decisions based solely on marketplace factors such as price and convenience?

• **Make a list of five people in business you admire because of their values.** List how your actions reflect your values throughout your work day and family life.

Chapter 7
What Makes Direct Sales/Multilevel Marketing Different?

SeneGence has given me the opportunity to become part of an extensive sorority of experts, intelligent business people, committed advocates of a great product, and basically "great people" — all set on building a business and being successful in direct sales/multilevel marketing. I have been privileged and honored to have been mentored and trained by a giant in the direct-selling cosmetics industry, a titan of home businesses, and a great lady: Ms. Joni Rogers-Kante! I am proud to have worked in a SeneGence world that brings beauty and self-esteem to women across our great country.

— KAROLE LEWIS, SeneGence Independent Distributor (Royal) and New York State Leader

Women who choose a career in direct sales have their own reasons for making that commitment. For some, it's frustration with a career going nowhere. For others, it's the need to find a way of making a living that allows you to also have a life, time at home and time with children.

It might be a way to earn more money during difficult times. Or it might be a way to be your own boss and determine the level of income you want to make.

My own choice to pursue a career in direct sales was based on many of those same reasons. I was looking for an opportunity to build a business modeled after the founders of Sav-On Drugs. I enjoyed the retail environment, but I felt limited by working always for somebody else. I wanted to be the owner of my own Sav-On Drugs, so to speak. I thought, "If I'm going to work so many hours and devote so much of my life energy to my business, why can't I own that business and pass it on to my heirs?"

So in 1980, at 22 years old, I searched for a pre-existing structure that would allow me to build my own business. At the time, for me, the answer was Mary Kay Cosmetics.

Selling cosmetics just seemed the right fit – an industry with which I was already familiar and to which I was powerfully attracted (for reasons not yet realized). It was a business populated with women. I thought that's probably where I had the best bet at success.

It was there I learned the business of direct sales. I learned that if you are looking for a career in a business, with a structure already in place, direct sales is the right place. In direct sales you don't have to recreate the wheel. You can take your energy and apply it to the money-making functions of building a business, because somebody else has already handled the overhead and the public relations and the marketing and the structure and the operations that are required to build a brand.

So you get to focus on simply marketing and, at least at SeneGence, training a sales force. And of course you get to focus on selling.

Once I started building my direct-sales business, I was learning how to be an entrepreneur, and I was thrilled to no longer be relying on a minimal paycheck every two weeks – although I was making a very good income at the time considering my age. I was placing a bet on me – that I could generate my own income and determine for myself the amount I should earn, without having a boss tell me what to do or how much I was worth.

Once I got started, I thought that particular direct-sales business was going to be my lifelong career, so I put everything I had to give into it. I learned how to build a downline, how to successfully support and mentor, how to demo and how to take good care of customers.

For the next few years I learned, sold, built an organization, developed and mentored downline leaders, and began to imagine how it would look if I were to start anew with a company designed for, well, me.

Learning all aspects of direct sales became my way of life for those years. I was working hard with other managers, planning events to build our business and conducting monthly trainings. I was the first director at Mary Kay to lease a "training center" where area directors could gather with their downlines, rotating trainings on the various days of the week.

We also held quarterly area events that supported the entire group of various downlines. It was magical. The results were outstanding. I was working with all of my downlines to help grow their businesses. My social life was based around my personal and business life at Mary Kay.

I was fully engaged in the "direct sales lifestyle."

I was learning that I was right for direct sales and that there were lots of other women who also were just right for direct sales, even though they were very different from me. I learned that very few women have a place to learn good business practices, and that's where I fit in perfectly – helping develop others into leaders.

There is no certain type of personality that fits perfectly into the direct-sales/multilevel marketing lifestyle. It takes all kinds.

Look at SeneGence or any other successful direct sales/multilevel marketing company, and see who rises to the top of the "sales ladder." You'll find very analytical sales superstars, very driven sales superstars, very animated sales superstars and very supportive-type sales superstars.

Although each is different, each has learned to orchestrate and blend with *different* personalities to help make those women successful and reach all the way to the top. Two ideas become evident: It takes a village to make a woman successful, and you must help others succeed before it is possible for you to succeed.

There are many reasons people are attracted to direct sales. Some come for money. Some want the freedom. Some join for retirement income, for security, for time, for travel, for recognition, for rewards. It's all there. At least if you are in the right direct-sales organization it is all there, and the best companies have rewards for each personality type.

There is one thing I remember from my business studies at junior college in Ventura, California: The highest paid, most successful managers have learned to successfully blend processes and people to achieve an end result. It is mixing support from the various personalities that are attracted to this business, meshing them together well, that allows you in the end to achieve your financial goals.

That's what being a successful manager is all about: meshing different kinds of people together using tools and processes needed to accomplish a common goal and achieve a desired end result.

I also learned that there are great opportunities in direct sales/multilevel marketing, and there are some opportunities that are not so great. In my estimation, there are two essential characteristics a direct-selling company must offer for it to truly be an excellent opportunity for prosperity: a great marketing plan that rewards focused effort, and a great product line.

Usually, one or the other aspect, a great marketing plan or a great product line, predominates. A truly outstanding company offers both!

At SeneGence, we offer both: A product line that really works and a career path that really works. So you can make extraordinary income with our company, selling great products that women really want.

The real key to success in our company as a Distributor is not just about reaping the rewards of our great sales-income earning potential of our great products. It's meshing the people and the processes together to exponentially multiply the returns 10, or 100, or 1,000 times more by helping each of our downline Distributors achieve her sales and growth goals and, in doing so, also earning commission income.

Real success also comes through meshing the various aspects of our business, from sales to sponsoring and everything else in between.

But above all else is sponsoring and mentoring others. If you sponsor as many new distributors as you sell products, you will without a doubt (remember faith?) become wealthy beyond your dreams.

That's especially true at SeneGence. There is no other company that has ever had the combination of the product line and the marketing plan that really works. And chances are if you're reading this book you already know this, or you're about to find out that SeneGence is probably the company, products and compensation plan for you too.

Do you want to test yourself to determine if this business is right for you? Let me ask you a few questions:

Are you self-motivated? Will you get out of bed, start moving on your own, learn and then engage in the actions that will make your day a successful and prosperous one – all without a boss telling you what to do?

Or are you the type of person who relies on an alarm clock to wake you up, watches clocks all day to determine when you're supposed to be at work because that's what is demanded of you, and when you get to work you want someone to tell you what it is that you're supposed to achieve that day before you can return home?

If you say you're that second kind of person I would highly recommend you stay with your current employer!

But if you are willing to change, then consider sticking your toe in direct sales by starting out very part time. Give yourself some time to determine if you want to develop the skills, to take your destiny into your own hands, to determine if you are a good boss to yourself and if you like the challenge of personal growth and development. Be kind to yourself. Allow for trial and error.

If, over the course of a year of giving direct sales your part-time attention, you find you have accomplished nothing, you didn't enjoy it, it's not for you ... well, you've lost nothing and probably made a few dollars and a few new friends (not to mention savings through tax deductions).

But maybe over the course of the year you find you're enjoying yourself in this new part-time career and you've developed some new skills and talents you didn't know you had. You had the chance to meet new friends, travel at least to new homes, towns or even to Seminars. You probably earned extra money too (again, not to mention the savings through tax deductions!). Then why not give yourself another year?

The point is, you don't have to jump into direct sales and become a record breaker in five years. You can enter direct sales at any commitment level. As they say, "To thine own self be true." Start where you are and progress year after year.

But suppose you are the first type of person described earlier. You're self-motivated, self-confident and self-directed. You're tired of working hard so someone else can profit.

My advice to you: Quit your job! Burn your bridges! Why are you working for someone else? Work for yourself!

What say you?

You probably think I misspoke. You're thinking, "Isn't the saying supposed to be '*Don't* burn your bridges?'"

No!

I still remember a pivotal moment when I spoke with Dad Jerry some 30 years ago about my frustrations with school (college business classes that I thought were outdated and a waste of my time) and my desire to pursue my own business. Dad shared with me some profound wisdom as I pondered leaving Sav-On Drugs. He said: "Joni, you are going to leave here (Sav-On Drugs) and chart your own course, so *burn your bridges* behind you. Then you have no choice other than to move forward."

Dad explained to me that if I *didn't* burn my bridges, in a moment of weakness or insecurity I would turn and retreat because going back across those bridges would seem the safest route. On the other hand, if there were no back-up plan (which there wasn't) I'd have to learn what it takes to succeed, and then try over and over again until I got it right in order to achieve the desired end result.

I am grateful to Dad Jerry for encouraging me in that moment to write a spirited letter of resignation that I then sent to Sav-On Drugs headquarters for all to see. There was definitely no turning back after that.

And I do not doubt the wisdom of that direction in which Dad helped me turn.

I am proud to say that almost a year later Sav-On executive Dennis Palmer, son-in-law of the company founder, spoke at my direct-sales event debut with Mary Kay. Dennis appeared as a keynote speaker at the request of Dad, who was out of the country at the time.

It was a magnificent event – the largest in the Los Angeles area to that date. Hundreds gathered at a hotel near Los Angeles International Airport to help me celebrate the achievements of my downline organization and the new benchmarks we set for the cosmetics company. VIPs from the company flew in; national sales directors attended. It was a true red-carpet event and a "defining moment" in my young life.

"Defining Moments," (similar to "destiny moments," see Page 23) are milestone moments and events we experience in our lives. At SeneGence we try to recognize "defining moments" or "moments in time" for every top achiever in our company each year at Seminar, year after year. Isn't that an appropriate way to celebrate a successful year of accomplishments?

So again, as Dad suggested to me, *"Burn your bridges!"* Why not invest in yourself? That's the safest investment you can ever make in someone. If, of course, you can count on yourself.

Can you count on yourself? Hopefully you can. If not, but you'd *like* to, continue developing the background support you need. Continue to build your direct-sales business part time, if necessary, until you build a customer base large enough to sustain yourself financially in reorders alone every month and even bypass your monthly income. Then you will be ready to step away from a full time "j.o.b."

Once you know you've arrived, you're building your business, trust yourself, are self-motivated and ready to break free, you can resign from that 40-hour "j.o.b." Now you are ready to commit 40 hours a week to developing your business. Your time has come.

By now you know you belong in direct sales. You're willing to go out there and "wow" others at street fairs, local networking events, social gatherings, church, parties, sports events, wherever. You know how to schedule business activities and your time. Why would you do that for anyone else? You belong in direct sales. It still surprises me that so many women, and so many men, haven't yet realized this is a viable alternative to collecting a paycheck.

You can learn the skills that you need to develop for this kind of success. Take, for example, the skill of public speaking. I'm a very shy person myself. I live in a very small world. I don't talk to people when I'm out and about. I'm not even comfortable getting up and speaking in front of large groups.

I'm not great at public speaking, but it's part of the job description.

I've learned to do it and I've finally decided to become a master at it by taking classes and actually practicing.

Have I improved? We can judge the results together.

So if someone says they're shy, or they're not comfortable getting up and talking in front of groups, I say, "So am I!" But guess what? If you choose to be successful, then public speaking is a skill you will develop over time.

You learn it by doing it. You don't have to begin with talking to large groups of, say, 100 women. You start by simply sharing how exciting this product line is to one woman at a time, then two women at a time. The next thing you know, you're speaking to dozens of women at a church group, then you're speaking to hundreds of women at a SeneGence Seminar. That's how it works!

It's not about how you feel right now. Anyway, you can't always control how you feel. Your success in direct sales is based upon your drive and what you're willing to learn so you can obtain the ultimate vision of your future.

People are not born into direct sales. People choose direct sales and then over years they learn the many skill sets required to become successful as their own bosses.

During one particularly challenging period of growth in my career I read a book for CEOs that said it takes at least 10 years of concentrated effort and practice to learn that job and become at least proficient at it.

My first thought was, "Whew (relief), I've still got a few years of practice to go ... with so much still to learn." *Good!*

Immediately, a light went on in my head and hope was restored to my heart as I realized I was learning a whole new set of skills; just as I had when learning direct-selling many years ago. Practice makes perfect. Daily, directed progress gets you closer to the ultimate perfection of the vision.

The way I see it, once you make a decision and commit yourself to that decision, there are three principles for success in direct-sales. They are "D.P.S.":

1. **Develop an attitude of success.**

2. **P**repare for and remain in a state of success; meaning develop success processes and support systems around you so that you are always in a state of success, and ...

3. Surround yourself with supportive people who encourage and support your success.

Let's look at each of these principles a little more closely.

First, "D" stands for developing an attitude of success. This is where you begin. Don't allow other people's reactions to affect your productivity. Have an attitude of "I will be successful at this regardless of how someone reacts." Learn to avoid the pitfall of acting out as a result of someone else's opinions. Someone else's attitude should have absolutely nothing to do with your state of mind and therefore your end result.

When I first started out sponsoring my "downline" as an independent beauty consultant with Mary Kay Cosmetics, the word "no" used to hurt my feelings. I would hear "no" – when a woman didn't want a facial or didn't want to become a consultant or just didn't want whatever I was offering, and I allowed that "no" to alter my future actions. I would stop prospecting for leads that day and become discouraged because that "no" was tough for me to deal with.

Eventually, at Mary Kay's suggestion, I learned to imagine I had an invisible shield around me, like a bubble, and I imagined those "no's" bouncing off the shield of the bubble. I imagined I was protected from negativity by that shield and therefore I could remain positive no matter what.

The imaginary shield worked for me, and it can work for you too!

The second principle, "P," stands for preparing *for* and remaining *in* a state of success. In other words, you must prepare for success in everything you do. As a SeneGence Independent Distributor you have to prepare your inventory levels so you can be as successful as possible when you conduct a Glamour Demo, right? The better prepared you are with adequate inventory, the more you sell through impulse purchases.

Another example: You have to prepare your desk to be organized and efficient so you are as successful as possible when sitting down making customer service reorder phone calls. And while making those reorder phone calls you are constantly planting "booking seeds" and "sponsoring seeds" to build future sales income and future commission income.

You also have to prepare the operations of your home so that you are not wasting time unnecessarily with housework when you should be focused on your business. Throw laundry in the washer and dishes in the dishwasher so you can make phone calls for an hour. Better yet, hire someone else to clean your home while you engage in recurring earning activities (remember Lee Iacocca's advice, Page 25).

That is what I mean by preparing for and staying in a state of success. Everything you do can result in maximizing the greatest return, because you are prepared.

Here's another big one: Preparing for the Glamour Demo. Why wouldn't you already have with you all of the inventory you could possibly sell at that demo? If you don't have the inventory on hand to support your selling, you're shooting yourself in the foot (Well, at least that's better than getting shot in the rear! See Chapter 1!) You're not making the money you *could* be making because you don't have what those customers need when they need it. There it is again: preparing for and staying in a state of success.

Put a portion of your profits to work, continuing in the cycle of inventory build-up using your customers' money (potential earnings!), especially in the beginning of your career.

Even the least experienced of us can realize the greatest success by learning the minute details and repetitive skill sets required to be successful.

Anyone can prepare for and stay in a state of success. Anyone can create an environment for opportunity. This point is vital. Preparing for and remaining in a state of success is required if you want "long-lasting" (no pun intended) success in direct sales or in any endeavor in life, for that matter.

That brings us to the *third* principle of success: "S" which stands for surrounding yourself with supportive people who encourage and support your success.

If you arrive home after a demo at night and your husband complains because the house is messy or the kids aren't in bed, and he asks something like "Why you are wasting your time playing cosmetics with the girls?" – Well, more than likely you have to ask yourself, "Why am I doing this and upsetting my husband?"

I'm not a marriage counselor. I've been happily married and I've been unhappily married. And by the way, the man I'm married to now, my beloved husband Ben, is the head of my household. I am *Mrs.* Kante at home. But sometimes women allow men to dominate them and their choices. I can't say that is wrong, but I can say if two people trying to build careers don't mesh, it is up to the woman to try to fix it, and "if you can't fix it, get rid of it." That is, *if* it's important to you to have your own career.

If your husband doesn't support your business, why not try engaging him in the process of helping you build it? In fact, bring him to me, let me show him what is possible and determine if your SeneGence success is a benefit to him in his life. Better yet, talk to him about the mortgage payment or rent payment, and see if that's important to him.

I mean, how difficult is it for a SeneGence Independent Distributor to make the mortgage payment? Think about it. One or two demos a week and you could be making the mortgage payment! How much pressure would that eliminate for *your* loved one? That's huge!

I'll bet that if you start paying the mortgage he'll pack your inventory bags for you, load them in the car, watch the kids, fix dinner and give you a big kiss when you return home from the demo!

What's more, while your sales cover that mortgage payment on a monthly basis, you will also be getting residual income through reorders ... over and over and over again. Not to mention commission income from sales by new distributors. And as your business grows, your reorder income grows and so too does your downline commission income.

This is the unique promise of the business of direct sales. Now that you have won your husband's support, the next thing to do is recruit the "little ones" to the cause of your business. I suggest asking, "Okay children, what camp (or trip/clothes/concert/movie) would you like to go to this summer (weekend/spring break/summer vacation, etc.)? Because I will set aside, after every demo, $10 for the (fill in the blank) of your choice." Trust me, they'll begin to gather names of friends' moms and hunt down prospects at the grocery store for you.

It's a little more challenging with extended family and friends who aren't supportive of your business, especially if they are "Negative Nellies." My best advice is to tell them the truth – that you need them to be as supportive and positive as possible as your family members are working together to achieve mutual goals. If they are going to be negative or make "sideways" remarks, your time with them will have to be limited, at best.

Do not take personal calls during scheduled work hours. If someone simply calls to chat, tell that person that you'll call back after your workday. You cannot afford to allow someone else's lack of urgency or clarity to affect your day's positive results.

You do this because, as principle three says, it's important to surround yourself with people who support your success.

In my experience, 99 percent of the women who come into this business come in not knowing what to do. Most don't have the previous experience, haven't yet learned how to build support, or simply just don't know the first steps to take.

Direct sales involves a 5- to 10-year learning cycle that, if followed, pays off like no other (legal) opportunity. There are many moving parts to it. Take time to get to know yourself and your strengths and what you feel you need to learn. It takes time to figure all of that out. Be kind to yourself, you can't learn it all in a year. Once you become an expert in direct sales, you've become an entrepreneur! Congratulations!

Why do some direct-sales entrepreneurs fail?

The biggest challenge for women in direct sales is, well, themselves. Women can cycle through emotions that are higher than a kite or lower than a snake. It may take a woman a year to complete a cycle, or it might happen 20 times a day.

Women's emotions turn up and down frequently, so there is a perception that women are erratic and can't be trusted to make day-to-day business decisions. We know that's not necessarily true for every woman, but maybe there is a kernel of truth behind the perception.

Here's an example:

A husband and a wife have a small disagreement before he leaves for work in the morning. The moment he steps foot from the house and into his car, his mind turns to traffic and then to the duties of the day, perusing his targeted goals. His day is challenging but flies by quickly as he accomplishes one objective after another. Before he knows it, it's time to head home. He gets in the car and his mind turns to eating his favorite meal, meatloaf, and perhaps a romp with the kids before their bedtime. After that, he's looking forward to spending a little time alone with his loved one to bring her up to speed with the day's events.

On the other hand, the experience of the same day for the wife is quite different. She was still stewing over the disagreement and exchange of words well into the late morning hours. While grocery shopping she intentionally did not speak about her products when a woman at the cash register noticed the SeneGence color samples on her hand and asked about them. Our wife/Independent Distributor responded by simply saying, "Yes, I was dabbling with makeup." She was in such a bad mood and preoccupied that she missed this perfect opportunity to grow her business.

Her day continues in this manner – missed opportunities with the girls at lunch, all of whom were using old-fashioned tube lipsticks. She didn't say a word to the hard-working waitress whose lipstick had worn off hours before (and who could have changed the course of her life by becoming a SeneGence Independent Distributor, beginning with part-time income). Finally, while picking up the kids at school our wife/Independent

Distributor quickly gathered the children into the car, missing the opportunity to invite one or more of the other mothers over to her "Mocha and Makeup" session during school hours.

By the time hubby arrived home, our wife/Independent Distributor was exhausted as a result of her brooding, feeling bad about her lack of progress, frustrated that she's not moving ahead in her career and doubting she chose the right career in the first place. Why? All because of her EMOTIONS!

She carried the morning disagreement with her throughout the morning and afternoon, which caused her to have a "brooding day" instead of a productive one like her husband's. Drat!

Here's how to overcome the depleting effects of situations such as this: *Learn to compartmentalize!*

I promise, if you learn to compartmentalize you will begin to clearly focus upon your objectives, giving 100 percent to scheduled and varied activities throughout the day, delivering the goods (achieving the goal) in a consistent manner and much, much more.

Men seem to be great at compartmentalizing. That's why when hubby walked out the door on his way to work, he still had a great day. His mind was in the "task-mode." He wasn't brooding over the morning disagreement.

I'm not sure where men learn to compartmentalize, but here's how I learned it ...

At age 15 I flew from Oklahoma, where I was living with Dad Bill Rogers, to California, where I moved in with my mother, JoAnn. My mother happened to be married to a man I called "Mr. Sav-On," Dad Jerry. As I've described in earlier pages of this book, my life then consisted of going to school, working at Sav-On Drugs after school, and getting to know a little about my new family over the course of the next three years while living at their house.

As it worked out, I saw my mother and sisters only fleetingly over those years, and the majority of my time was spent at work with "Mr. Sav-On."

During the day Mom and Dad morphed into a professional "power couple." Mom was an office coordinator and Dad was a busy executive at Sav-On. During the day, it was "Yes m'am" and "No, sir," and no messing around. I was treated hard, worked harder, and expected to act more professionally than other employees. No "Mommy" and "Daddy" at work. However, once "Mr. and Mrs. Sav-On" walked through the front door at home, well, Mom and Dad were back! I spent most evenings curled up on the couch, chatting with Dad, lounging in his recliner, talking about all types of business issues and ethics. I still cherish those discussions.

From this experience I learned first-hand about compartmentalization. It is a good thing and a very productive way to get through the day; to be efficient at all of the activities required in a busy life, and still be there fully for family in the non-work hours.

Add this skill to a well-arranged weekly schedule, and you can definitely achieve your dreams! You just need time and focus.

Learn to be consistent in your decision-making processes and in the way you judge and hear things. Learn this, and you will be able to make the direct-sales journey from beginning to end without unnecessarily spending twice the emotional energy required. But if you're emotionally up and down all the time, you may get very tired, worn out, and doubting your career choices.

You can bet that every successful SeneGence Queen and Crown Princess (our two highest levels) has mastered the skill of compartmentalization. SeneGence Queen Jeri Taylor-Swade is a perfect example. Jeri is a very emotional and inspiring woman, but when you look closer you see she's very consistent in her decision-making processes and has made it through some very challenging situations. She has learned how to compartmentalize. I have great admiration for her, and so should you.

❧ Your Turn (Chapter 7) ☙

• Experience has shown that many different personality types are capable of incredible success in sales-based businesses. By knowing your own type, you can build on your strengths and also learn how to incorporate elements of the other types into your personality, making you even stronger as a sales professional by rounding out your personality. **Which basic type are you?**

a) Analytical – You naturally are drawn to sales projections, returns on investment, etc. And you thoroughly understand product features and how they link to specific benefits. You're a *thinker and can help those members of the team who are not.*

b) Highly Driven – You are the one who is willing to work harder than everyone else around you to get the prize, whether it's in sales and sponsoring or in other areas of your life. You're a *competitor and you inspire others members of the team to reach for more along with you.*

c) Animated – You have a passion for products and for making your customers' lives better. You fully engage your emotions and your bodily expressions in your sales and sponsoring presentation. You're a *persuader and influence other members of the team.*

d) Supportive – You are the embodiment of consultative selling and sponsoring: You get involved in your customers' and downline distributors' lives and find solutions through empathy and caring. You're a *nurturer who helps other members of the team to success.*

Your Turn (Chapter 7 cont'd)

This list isn't complete, but you get the idea: First figure out who you are and then build from there. Note that it takes all four personality types to build a well-balanced and effective team.

• One of the most important business lessons I ever received from my Dad was to "Burn Your Bridges!" When he first told me this, I did a double-take, I thought I heard it wrong. But then I realized Dad was talking about the bridges in our lives we are afraid to cross fully and move from one side of the bridge to the other and beyond. For me, that "burning bridges" took the form of a resignation letter to my employer. The "bridge" keeps us stuck in the past because we know we can always retreat back to where we came from. **Can you think of three examples in your own life and career in which you are afraid to "burn bridges" and let the past go?** Maybe it's a bad career choice from the past that keeps you "stuck" on one side of the bridge? Or maybe it's that nagging self-doubt that somebody around you has embedded in your thoughts or words; words that have stuck in your head since when you were young? Maybe it's time for you to "burn your bridges" and move forward.

Resolve to burn your bridges. Make of list of bridges you will "torch." Note how you will do it, what has to happen, how you are going to make that happen; and by what date you will put a match to the bridge!

Chapter 8
What Do You *Really* Want?

Positivity and negativity are like the forces of good and evil. Positivity dispenses evil, and vice versa. Choose sides. Choose positivity.

— JONI

Before setting goals in life and in business, you must identify what your Goal (with a capital G) really is and why you want it.

Start by asking yourself: "What do I want out of life?" Then ask more questions.

Do you want more income? Well, *why* do you want more income? Is it so you will be free from worries and can spend more time raising and nurturing your children? Now you are getting closer to what you really want and why you want it. Is it to create a life and a legacy that will continue to nourish and support your children and your grandchildren even after you are gone?

To me, that's beginning to sound like a Goal you really want!

You see, those "Goals" are a lot bigger than buying a new home or taking a trip or even working less while making more or becoming more fulfilled as a spiritual person. Ultimately the big "Goal" should direct all the little goals you set in life. These little goals are stepping stones to the big Goal.

My big Goal is – and has been for a long time – to create a worldwide, solid, sustainable, ethical company that "I can pass on to my children." This Goal directs every single action I undertake as the CEO of SeneGence. I weigh and measure the benefits of short-term and long-term goals in the context of my Goal.

Business decisions, for me, aren't necessarily about how our company might make the most money, or grow most quickly, or become the largest in our industry, or one of a hundred other considerations. I focus on building a worldwide, solid, sustainable, ethical company, while serving a "higher purpose" that I can pass on to my children; a company that's built in a way to sustain them and their children should they choose. And, in turn, so too will our Distributors and their children benefit in the same manner.

Often, it's my focus on the Goal that has given the strength to move forward through tough business and personal times. And that's one of the most important things about having the Goal. It helps you stay focused when your negative thoughts are telling you to quit or to compromise.

Once you determine what your real Goal is in life, or at least in business, you can then begin working on setting and accomplishing short-term goals and objectives that will move you forward in the right direction to achieve the real Goal. It's a great idea to write your real Goal or Goals down on a piece of paper and carry that paper in your wallet. Then, several times a week, read the Goals to yourself to stay focused. Remember what Dad Jerry told me: "What we think about is what we become."

Just as important as identifying the real Goal: You've got to have the right attitude as you begin your journey at work and elsewhere in life.

Your attitude will make or break your ability to achieve your goals – short term, long term and especially the real Goal. It all boils down to maintaining a positive attitude regardless of the situation. A positive attitude is an absolute requirement for success in direct sales, as in any business – particularly because this is a people business and people in general like to befriend and associate with positive people.

The great illustration of this is in the book *Think and Grow Rich* by inspirational writer Napoleon Hill. It's the story of a miner whom Hills refers to as R.U. Darby, an East Coast merchant who came west to strike it rich mining for gold during the Gold Rush of the 19th Century. This is a very popular story among direct-sales superstars, and I urge you to listen carefully. The story, as Hill told it, is called "Three

Feet From Gold." It goes like this:

"An uncle of R. U. Darby was caught by the "gold fever" in the gold-rush days, and went west to DIG AND GROW RICH. He had never heard that more gold has been mined from the brains of men than has ever been taken from the earth. He staked a claim and went to work with pick and shovel. The going was hard, but his lust for gold was definite.

After weeks of labor, he was rewarded by the discovery of the shining ore. He needed machinery to bring the ore to the surface. Quietly, he covered up the mine, retraced his footsteps to his home in Williamsburg, Maryland, told his relatives and a few neighbors of the "strike." They got together money for the needed machinery, had it shipped. The uncle and Darby went back to work the mine.

The first car of ore was mined, and shipped to a smelter. The returns proved they had one of the richest mines in Colorado! A few more cars of that ore would clear the debts. Then would come the big killing in profits.

Down went the drills! Up went the hopes of Darby and Uncle! Then something happened! The vein of gold ore disappeared! They had come to the end of the rainbow, and the pot of gold was no longer there! They drilled on, desperately trying to pick up the vein again—all to no avail.

Finally, they decided to QUIT.

They sold the machinery to a junk man for a few hundred dollars, and took the train back home. Some "junk" men are dumb, but not this one! He called in a mining engineer to look at the mine and do a little calculating. The engineer advised that the project had failed, because the owners were not familiar with "fault lines." His calculations showed that the vein would be found JUST THREE FEET FROM WHERE THE DARBYS HAD STOPPED DRILLING! That is exactly where it was found!

The "Junk" man took millions of dollars in ore from the mine, because he knew enough to seek expert counsel before giving up."

I believe that positivity and negativity are like the forces of good and evil. Positivity dispenses evil and vice versa. Choose sides. Stand for one or the other. Choose positivity to build goodness.

Do not let evil/negativity win. It will prevent you from achieving your real Goal, and it will subvert your shorter-term goals and objectives at every step along the way, making it impossible to achieve a positive outcome. Make a commitment right here and now, as you read these words, to always maintain a positive attitude and you will be on your way to building goodness and getting what you REALLY want in life and in business.

To that end, I offer these tips I have picked up along the way in my life and career. They may help you to maintain a positive attitude:

1. **Eliminate negativity from your life.** Are the people around you filling you with positive thoughts? Are they supportive of your wishes, of your real Goal? Surround yourself with positive thinkers; they will cheer you on and will allow you the freedom to achieve your goals and even lend a hand. Distance yourself from negative influencers: they will intentionally try to discourage you from achieving your goals. Be compassionate toward your negative friends and family members; they are not comfortable with change and progress. And they don't realize what influences they are projecting. Try to understand their discomfort. Eventually, they will learn that their negativity falls on deaf ears when speaking with you as their comments simply no longer affect your state of mind, attitude or actions. You will be teaching them an important lesson about how to develop a positive attitude.

2. **Work persistently and consistently toward each goal.** Remember Napoleon Hill's story about the persistent gold miner. What you think about, you bring about. Your consistent, positive actions and thoughts will manifest themselves, drawing you closer and closer to your goals. There are many, many training programs that focus on how your thoughts are in essence merged with the energy of the universe. Thoughts alone can drive all

that you desire to you, to achieve your dreams. Read Deepak Chopra for more information.

Use a datebook. A datebook should be an essential success tool you use every day to stay on track and focused. Schedule time with family and work appointments, before scheduling other appointments. Note which appointments can accomplish more than one task at a time; e.g., lunch with a girlfriend can also serve as a wowing opportunity to build business and a chance to run errands before and after the scheduled appointment. Of course, as you are running errands you are also encountering entirely new wowing opportunities.

3. **Keep smiling.** The physical act of smiling sends a message to your unconscious mind. *The New York Times* says it takes 10 facial muscles to smile and 100 to frown. Not only is smiling easier, but it produces results. Men, women and children prefer the company of those who smile far more than the company of those who do not. Smile when you answer the phone. Try it! The caller will "see" you smiling. They will hear it in your voice. Place a mirror on your desk near the phone and smile at yourself. You'll feel better too!

4. **Adopt a "never give up" strategy.** I've heard the story of Henry Ford telling his engineers he wanted them to invent the V-8 engine. They said it couldn't be done. He sent his engineers back to the design labs to keep working on it. They came back and again said it can't be done. So Henry Ford told them to keep working on it anyway, since they were being paid, and they went back again convinced it couldn't work. Suddenly, they achieved an engineering solution and within no time the world's first successful V-8 engine was designed and ready for

production. So learn a lesson: Make a commitment to your goals and never give up.

There's another story I have heard from many: You can't make a great lip color and cosmetic line with color that stays on all day and at the same time makes your skin more beautiful. Well, I guess we proved otherwise, didn't we girls?

5. **Eliminate fear.** "Know thyself," said the oracle at Delphi. Most of your fears are learned, and you can unlearn them starting now. I used to be afraid of tarantulas. I still don't particularly like them, but I am no longer afraid of them. Identify your fears. List them on paper. Set about learning how to eliminate them. Read self-help books. Attend self-help seminars.

My Dad Bill was a paratrooper at one point during his stint as a U.S. Marine. But the thought of jumping out of a plane at 10,000 feet made me queasy. So I decided to overcome that fear. Ben and I took the entire SeneGence staff to Perris, California, for a "dive."

Some chose to dive in tandem, attached to an experienced skydiver. Ben and I, in character, decided we'd both dive solo after a few hours of instruction. Everyone had an exhilarating experience and safely returned to the ground ... except Ben and me. He ended up with a broken tail bone and I wound up with a broken rib. That's what happens when you crash into the cement wall of a water canal face-forward, and then slide down into a thorny bush patch! Michael Moad, our company president and chief legal officer, will no longer allow company "dive" trips. The good news is I am no longer afraid of skydiving. But I wouldn't do it again!

Make a commitment to grow and to eliminate unwarranted fears that hold you back from experiencing a full life. This will probably be a long process, so be willing to start now, right where you are. And have fun overcoming your fears.

6. **Continue your education.** School is never out for a professional. Learn your trade. Learn more about network marketing and direct sales. If you're a SeneGence Independent Distributor, study up on color cosmetics and skin care. Check out course listings at your local community college or trade school. Study what it takes to be a successful entrepreneur. Knowledge is power, and it builds confidence. I've found that because there is so much I don't know, I have had to resort to scheduling one hour a day for "education" during work hours just so I could ensure I made the time to actually do it. I look forward to that period of one hour every day.

7. **Accept "problems" as your friends.** Solving problems is like building a bridge. Once the bridge is built it provides the road that brings you closer to the solution, toward your Goal. Visualize problems as exercises to keep your brain strong. They really do! Studies have shown that mental exercises actually lessen the effects of Alzheimer's disease and improve cognition at all ages. Think about the advice you get at the gym: Persistence and commitment to a training program, with gradual increases in resistance, build muscle. So think of your problems and frustrations as a workout. Solving a problem gives your mind a workout and strength to deal with the next problem, and with exercise (experience) problem solving becomes a breeze and a fun challenge, like a game.

8. **Look professional at all times.** Look polished and successful at work, play and during leisure time. You never know whom you may bump into. This is doubly important in the cosmetics and beauty industry. For SeneGence Independent Distributors, always, always, always wear your long-lasting color of SenseCosmetics and use Anti-Aging SeneDerm Skincare every day. Remember, you are a walking billboard for your business.

9. **Know that you are a very special being.** You were put here on Earth to make a contribution. I know this without a doubt. Your contributions are captured in your dreams. If you have dreams, you have the ability to achieve your dreams. Believe in your abilities. Don't compare yourself to anyone. Ever. Allow yourself room to grow and to make mistakes. I've made plenty of them! Be kind to yourself when you fail from time to time.

I fail, learn from it, turn toward another direction and move forward. The good thing about failing is learning that what you were doing is not the way to proceed. So, evaluate alternatives and, when necessary, change direction. Continue to choose and move for results. If necessary, choose and move again. It's a cycle that brings about success. Every successful person I know goes through this cycle. They know it's the cycle and the way to figure out success, and therefore they are not discouraged nor do they give up when they do not achieve their desired outcome. Remember, "If you do not succeed at first ... try, try again."

Get back up. Smile. Go forth. You have much to accomplish. I know you can achieve what you really want. I know you will.

≋ Your Turn (Chapter 8) ≋

• **What does the story "Three Feet From Gold" mean to you?** What quality do you think the "junk man," who hired an expert to help him, had that Darby and his uncle lacked? Write your own moral for the story, in 15 words or fewer. Then consider taping your "moral" on your bathroom mirror, where it can remind you every morning of what it takes to be a sales and sponsoring superstar.

Take time to ponder what life would look like for you today had you not quit some particular project before completion. Resolve to yourself to *always* complete projects, as the completion of one project after another builds into a "life's work."

• **Take a moment to review the nine tips outlined in this chapter on developing and maintaining a positive attitude.** Pick the three that resonate most strongly with you, and write a short list of actions you will take in the next week to improve in each of those three areas: For example, for #3, "Keep Smiling," list three specific situations in which you tend to be unhappy and then see if you can't practice smiling through those same situations this week.

• Smile right now. **Smile big.** How does it feel?

Chapter 9
Dancing with the Stars:
Eight Steps to a Successful Direct-Sales Career

The moment I started at SeneGence I knew that this was going to be my avenue to help empower other women. When you're working for yourself, you need to have a grasp of what keeps you motivated. Being in business for myself but also with such a great affiliation with this company, I feel as if I have the best of both worlds. Since I joined SeneGence, I've learned to take charge, get out and do things. It's been a very empowering experience and I believe we haven't even scratched the surface of this company's potential.

— KATIE SEVENANTS, SeneGence Independent Distributor (Royal and Washington State Leader)

I am going to teach you how you could make approximately $35,000 a year working about 10 hours a week. Work about 20 hours a week and you could double that amount. Work a 40-hour week and you could easily make around $140,000 a year and more – simply by mastering the "Direct Sales Dance."

You may not believe me yet, but after you try this approach you will believe it.

There are eight fundamental dance "steps" that you must master to do the Direct Sales Dance and be successful as a direct-sales entrepreneur. In direct sales, you have no boss and no annual review. That makes you the "lead" dancer. Whether or not you are accomplishing your objectives will be demonstrated by the financial rewards you reap at the end of each year.

There's no entrance exam or previous required work experience. You simply have to be willing to learn these eight steps the very best you can, given your individual level of commitment to your direct-sales business.

The eight dance steps are: Wowing, Booking, Demo-ing, Directing, Sponsoring, Customer Service, Training and Ongoing Education.

Remember what Lee Iacocca said about focusing your time and energy on the activities that return the most to your business income? The first four steps in our list of eight will ensure you are properly focused on money-making activities, not just busy work. So do them first, and make sure you include those four basic activities – wowing, booking, demo-ing and directing – in your weekly schedule and you will make handsome profits in your direct-sales business.

It sounds simple and it is simple. But I can't even begin to count the many, many women who do not follow this simple blueprint for building a career. They insist on sidestepping, which usually means dancing the wowing and demo-ing steps and not much else. They are two-stepping and sidestepping instead of eight-stepping. And they two-step right off the dance floor and out the door – never to be seen or heard from again!

But if you want to do the Direct Sales Dance successfully you must commit to all eight steps in this business process. Not just your favorite two or three steps.

Let's go through them together in a little more detail in the order of activities that result in the most effective outcome – and income. By the way, I'll be talking specifically using SeneGence terms, but you can apply these steps to almost all direct sales opportunities.

1. **Wowing**: Developing new business prospects by engaging others in trying the product. There are dozens of fun and creative ways to do this every day, every month, every occasion throughout the year.

2. **Booking**: Calling leads to book appointments for single and group demonstrations, open houses, trunk parties, fairs, women's events, networking gatherings, etc.

3. **Demonstrating** (we call it "Glamour Demo-ing"): Holding the product event, with those with whom you booked appointments, teaching women about product technologies and how to use/apply the product.

4. **Directing**: Giving every attendee at the Glamour Demo the choice to become a customer or a new distributor. You then spend time directing those who choose to become your customers through the customer support systems of "SeneService" and selling these products at retail. Meanwhile you direct those who choose to become Distributors through the "SeneSentials" training program for Distributors, and help them place orders for products at a discount directly from the company, upon which you receive commissions.

5. **Sponsoring**: Signing up and training new Distributors to whom you have demonstrated the products, and learning skills that help you increase the number of women sponsored, ultimately increasing commission income earnings.

6. **Customer Service**: Calling customers and learning skills that will help you maximize customer value, partner for profit and conduct various sales events on their behalf. This also includes the dozens of other ways you can offer ongoing involvement that allows them to earn or purchase reorder products, promotions, sales, etc., resulting in increased sales income.

7. **Training**: Attending weekly or monthly company trainings and events. SeneGence sponsors formal training on a weekly, monthly, quarterly and annual basis to help teach Distributors all aspects of the SeneGence career.

8. **Education**: Reading training manuals and self-help books, attending classes, Seminars and other events that apply to your business interests. This is a lifelong learning process.

As I said, the first four steps are the most important. Just do them and you will prosper. It doesn't take a lot of work. Use your own style and grace.

Have fun with it and let your inner self shine through. Don't try to be perfect. I've yet to conduct a perfect Glamour Demo, and I've been doing this a long time!

You could make about $35,000 a year if you commit to generating 10 new prospects a week from any variations of wowing you will learn. Those 10 new names/prospects will yield an average of five bookings for glamour demonstrations that you conduct for one or more women (the more women, the more money). I have seen this work for more than 20 years.

It never fails, and I like that. You are the mistress of the outcome. Those five bookings will realistically result in two to three actual Glamour Demos held, because the other two or three will cancel or postpone before the appointed date. Don't worry, and don't take cancellations personally. It's to be expected. In fact, it seems to be a direct-sales law!

At the two or three demos each week, you will be demonstrating and teaching the features and benefits of the products. Offer each guest at the Glamour Demo an opportunity to purchase products right then and there as a customer at retail value, upon which you earn sales income. Offer to enroll them as SeneGence Independent Distributors, which will allow them to purchase their products directly from the company at a discount from suggested retail, in which case you will receive commission income. Remember, each woman who attends a SeneGence Glamour Demo, including your hostess, is a new name/prospect for you to "mine" for additional bookings for Glamour Demos. The success cycle continues from one booking to the next.

That's why I say focus on these four activities: 1) Wow for names/prospects, 2) Book demo appointments , 3) Conduct Glamour Demos, and 4) Direct each attendee to become either a customer or distributor. These are the activities that will empower you to become a very successful direct-sales entrepreneur.

Remember what I call the "10-5-2 Principle": 10 names/prospects per week will yield five booked Glamour Demos (of many types) of which two to three will actually hold.

Make that your dance routine, put your own personality into it, and you could earn approximately $35,000 a year or more working part time.

Step 4, Directing, enables you to view every woman who attends a Glamour Demo as a successful business experience. She chooses either to become a customer or she chooses to become a new Distributor. You know you have the best products in the marketplace, so why wouldn't every woman want to become a Distributor and share these products with every woman she knows? At Glamour Demos, look for your next new Distributor – the others will default to becoming customers.

Directing customers and Directing your Distributors is where your business really takes off. But to get to that point, you first engage in the first three dance steps: Wowing, Booking and Demo-ing. These three steps are all about selling first the idea of trying the product (Wowing), and secondly, selling the appointment. Thirdly, you are selling the product at the Glamour Demo by teaching its features and benefits.

Schedule time every week to "wow em!" Visit business offices, salons, spas, churches, doctors' offices and so on; wherever there may be women with lips and skin. Take with you a supply of company brochures, newsletters and other materials, making sure your name, ID Number, phone number and email address are on each. These tools can then be used in many ways.

Suppose you walk into an office and meet a receptionist. You offer to place a dot of lip color on her hand, as you tell her something like this:

"I represent a new color technology we like to market to working women because it truly lasts for hours, for the entire workday."

You rub the back of your own hand, where you have already applied several of the colors, then continue.

"We offer free glamour demonstrations with no obligation to purchase products. How many women work here? Well, I'll be happy to demonstrate this product line, free of charge, during a lunch break. I'll put a dot of this on the back of your hand. Show the other women and ask if they'd be interested in trying it. I'll call you tomorrow to determine what day of the week would be best for me to return for a Glamour Demonstration." Take her card and be sure to follow up. If she can't book a Glamour Demo at her place of work, perhaps one of the women in the office might volunteer her home after work hours.

You've just opened the door to unknown possibilities in sales, demos, booking and sponsoring opportunities.

The result of this kind of effort is a booked Glamour Demo. See how it flows?

Wowing leads to nowhere unless you actually book a Glamour Demo, so be sure to focus on booking Glamour Demos from leads gathered. Ask family and friends if you may talk to their managers or human resources departments to book group Glamour Demo presentations or to simply book a demo after hours at their homes.

Once you've booked the Glamour Demo, actually add a name, location and time for the Glamour Demo into your calendar. The next step is to conduct the Glamour Demo for all those women, who will be very grateful for the opportunity to learn about your incredible products and the opportunity that really works!

Double book time slots, if possible, to ensure you hold as many Glamour Demos each week as targeted. Life happens. People postpone and even cancel appointments for all kinds of reasons. If no one cancels in a double-booked time slot, choose which appointment you want to keep and give the other appointment to one of your first-line distributors whom you have sponsored, as you earn commissions on what that Distributor sells too. In return, your "first line" sends you 10 percent of their Glamour Demo profits as a "thank you" for the referral. Now that's working and earning smart!

Schedule multiple Glamour Demos every week. This will come as a result of your Wowing efforts, and eventually new bookings will be generated from current bookings. Allow three to four hours for each demonstration, including travel time to and from the event. Bring plenty of inventory to the Demo for impulse purchases. A full inventory at the time of the sale will eliminate wasted profits spent on postage, unproductive driving time delivering products, etc. Make sure you show all of the products you bring to the Glamour Demo.

Over and over in direct sales it has been proven that you will sell what you show. Be sure to pre-assemble or order sponsoring packets — a special packet for your future Glamour Demo hostesses (such as the receptionist you initially set the demo with). Bring Partner for Profit Paks and potential Distributor Paks to send home with any women who are interested but undecided ... and follow up for fantastic results. Be generous.

At your demo, also be sure to ask for referrals for additional Glamour Demos. Always, always, always make it easy for your prospects to purchase products or sign on as Distributors by introducing optional ways to pay. Be creative and build relationships that last by helping women get what they want. You too will prosper and you will soon be doing your Dance with the Stars!

≈ Your Turn (Chapter 9) ≈

• You can generate about $35,000 annual income in direct sales by starting with a commitment to find 10 new prospects every week. Whether you're already a direct-sales professional or not, try this timed exercise right now: Give yourself five minutes (use a stopwatch or cell phone to time yourself). **Now, write a list of 10 people you could invite to a product demonstration if you were trying to book one.** Your list can include family, friends, co-workers, neighbors or anyone else. If you are already working in direct sales, then use this as a real-life opportunity to identify additional leads. Ready? Set? Go!

• **Call every name on that list and get started towards success.** Right NOW!

Roots

My mother and I left the hospital for my grandparents' farm in Sapulpa, Oklahoma, shortly after this picture was taken a few days after I was born.

Mom, Dad, my brother Billy and I together on the front porch of our farmhouse.

Dad with all four children dressed up for a special occasion.

My father, William Rogers, and my brother Billy on the farm in Sapulpa, Oklahoma.

Roots cont'd

Playing Barbie as a young girl in Oklahoma.

Becoming a young lady on the farm in Sapulpa; Behind me is a real "cowbell" Mother Rogers used to call the children in at mealtime.

A photo of me on a bicycle a few years after a collision between me, on my tricycle, and a pickup truck led to a lifetime of guidance from my Heavenly Father.

At the airport in Oklahoma ready for a rare visit with sisters and Mother who lived in California.

Roots cont'd

My father, William, with Grandmother Rogers and Great-Great Grandmother Rogers in the kitchen of our farm home in Sapulpa, Oklahoma.

Maureen Dean, wife of Watergate defendant John Dean, inspired me in my childhood with her calm manner and simple, refined beauty under fire.

Me (Joni Rae) and Mary Kay Ash during training in Dallas, Texas.

Roots cont'd

Ben and I with Mentor Anthony Robbins looking at stunning lots with views in Namale, Fiji.

Speaking with SeneGence offices, prior to a daytime excursion to Mount Yasur, using satellite phone while at Camp Resolution in Vanuatu.

SeneGence

In black and white it's difficult to tell, but I was often wearing this favorite pink dress in the 1990s as I built my business with Mary Kay Cosmetics.

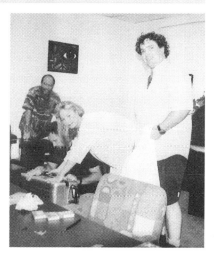

Ben and I staging equipment in SeneGence offices just before departing for Vanuatu.

Samples of volcanic ash and botanicals are loaded onto a boat in Vanuatu for shipment back to the U.S. on our exploratory trip in 2001.

SeneGence cont'd

Digging samples of volcanic ash at the base of Mount Yasur on Vanuatu. The volcanic ash was proven to contain skin-enhancing ingredients that are now included in many SeneGence products.

Top Distributors holding LipSense: Bottom row from left: Pattie Lambert, Pamela Bennett, Jeri Taylor-Swade, Lauren Syverud. Second row from left: Amber London, Teri White, Martha Geraghty, Flo Fischer, Karole Lewis. Third row from left: Kelly Robertson, Dawn Christian, Sheila Young Nicole Russell, Roxanne Kumasaka. Top row from left: Dody Furst, Michelle Aupperlee, Katie Sevenants, Deb Sell.

SeneGence cont'd

SeneGence Independent Distributors today can win cars on top of other rewards as "ManaGence" leaders. Field Leaders from left above: Dawn Christian, Bridget Lambrose, Sheila Young, Caroline Bishop, Me (Joni), Leslie Bradley, Zoanne Weaver, Anne Miner, Roxanne Kumasaka.

SeneGence cont'd

On stage at a SeneGence Seminar, sharing recognition with my leaders.

Last safety check prior to sky diving solo during a Senegence company outing with employees.

There is nothing as grand and motivating as an annual SeneGence Seminar, which gives SeneGence leaders a chance to be recognized onstage.

SeneGence cont'd

Today's technology makes training SeneGence Distributors around the world simple and fun for all. Pictured here training Senegence Distributors in Australia from SeneGence offices in Irvine Calif., are (from left) Queen Jeri Taylor-Swade, Leslie Bradley, and Me (Joni).

We often plan to take our SeneGence Leaders on fun three- and four-day trips like this one aboard a cruise liner while training ... and having fun, of course.

SeneGence cont'd

Speaking to early SeneGence Independent Distributors at the grand opening of SeneGence headquarters in Newport Beach in 2000.

The lobby also served as a Distributor training area in the first building SeneGence occupied, in Newport Beach, Calif.

SeneGence cont'd

Ultralux, the early lip-color product I sold to raise capital for our proprietary line of products beginning with LipSense.

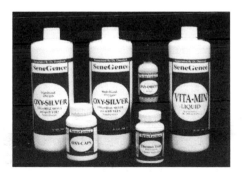

Early in SeneGence history we marketed a line of nutritional supplements developed by the well-known Dr. Kurt Donsbach.

Today the SeneGence product line includes an array of SenseCosmetics and SeneDerm Skincare products.

Family

My stepfather Jerry Hight, and my mother JoAnn at my wedding in 2004.

My precious family today includes my handsome son Alan, me, husband Ben and our beautiful young boy, William.

I pose with future husband Ben in a candid shot from our Vanuatu trip in 2000. It was Ben's loving guidance and engagement with my son Alan that convinced me Ben was the one for me!

Applying LipSense minutes before my marriage to Ben.

A nuptial kiss between Ben and I at our wedding at the Beverly Hills Hotel in May 2004.

Me with Carmen Holladay, my friend and supporter. I will be forever grateful for all she has done for me and my family.

Employees

My dear talented and versatile husband and friend, Ben Kante, SeneGence chief operations officer.

SeneGence President and guiding hand Michael Moad, who has done his best from the beginning to keep me out of hot water.

SeneGence Controller Melida Altman has watched over the finances of SeneGence with a cautious and discerning eye since the beginning.

Linda Bailey, our first SeneGence employee who started with us to answer the busy phones and has help us grow. Linda's long years in the field of law make her the perfect person to watch over our Compliance Department.

The living room became the warehouse in the trailer.

Nights were spent filling the original LipSense Glossy Gloss vials at the kitchen bar in the trailer.

Chapter 10
Sponsoring: Sharing (And Receiving) Wealth

Joni is a natural leader. She was always very popular and people just naturally look up to her. She is the kind of person who can fit well into any group and any class of people. She is so natural and unaffected that people just immediately feel comfortable around her. By the same token, she is one of the most driven people I have ever known. She has such an ability to focus that I wish I could be more like her. At first appearance, she comes off as being very independent. But I don't believe she's as independent as some people might think. She relies heavily on the people she cares about and has come to trust ... and I think that's a strength, not a weakness.

— KRISTIN WOOLERY, SeneGence Independent Distributor and childhood friend of Joni

In direct sales/multilevel marketing (MLM) you receive wealth to the extent that you share opportunities with others.

There are two ways that wealth is earned in direct sales/MLM: You either sell products, for which you are paid a commission, or you sponsor and manage other distributors who in turn sell products, in which case you get a smaller but still significant commission on *their* product sales. The key is to exponentially grow that commission by building a sales force upon which you earn huge commissions – far more that you could possibly earn by selling products all by your lonesome. Become a people person and prosper!

That's basically it. You either a) sell, or b) manage others you've sponsored doing the same thing.

"Sponsoring" is where the "multilevel marketing" part comes in. The first three steps in our eight-step process discussed in the last chapter were really all about direct sales. And you can be successful in direct sales by selling products to others, especially when you have a product that is as exciting as SeneGence SenseCosmetics and SeneDerm Skincare, which almost sell themselves.

You can make a pretty good living just selling products and doing all the things that selling requires: Wowing, booking, demo-ing, taking orders, customer service and so on.

But at that level you're only doing the "direct sales" part of direct sales/multilevel marketing. Sponsoring others into the organization is when the real opportunity comes in to play for you. That's why this business is not just direct sales; it's direct sales *and* multilevel marketing.

If you're new to direct sales and multilevel marketing, let me explain.

As a direct-sales professional, you purchase products at a wholesale price that is less than the suggested retail price. When you sell these products at Glamour Demos, parties, trade shows, or wherever, you earn sales income or "profits" that equal the difference between what you pay for the product at wholesale prices as a distributor and the price at which you sell the product (suggested retail), minus, of course, your overhead for travel, trade-show booths, selling supplies, etc. For SeneGence Independent Distributors, selling at home Glamour Demos offers the lowest overhead cost and often the greatest profits.

Figuring your cost of buying products from a direct-sales company plus overhead/business expenses, you might typically make 40 percent or 40 cents on every dollar of sales. So if you hold a product demo or party and sell 20 products at $20 each, you will have $400 in sales and thus $160 in profit for the three or four hours spent. Not bad, right?

But now imagine a large network of women you sponsored who are all out doing the same thing. Every time one of those women you sponsored conducts a Glamour Demo and makes a sale, she earns about 40 percent but you also earn 10 percent commission paid back directly to you from the company on each sale, accumulated every month. And you didn't have to do anything after you sponsored and trained your Distributor, or "downline." You may have earned that income while at the movies with your husband during date night.

Now let's suppose your downline Distributor at that Glamour Demo sponsors a new Distributor into her organization (and thus your organization). Not only will your downline Distributor begin earning 10 percent of that new Distributor's sales directly from the company, but you will receive 6 percent of the sale (assuming you meet qualifications) because she, the new Distributor, was sponsored by the woman *you* sponsored. And on it goes, down five levels from you. Though the percentage grows smaller as you move down your line, the return is generally larger due to exponential growth, and you are not working any harder to make that happen. It all begins with you wowing, booking, demoing and directing customers and Distributors.

Do the math, and you will see why so many men and women around the world build their careers in direct sales/multilevel marketing and make fortunes at it.

I like to think of sponsoring from two angles: the functional side of it – that is, how to sponsor others – and from the attitude side of it. If you approach the direct sales/MLM business with a "sponsoring attitude" you are almost certain to prosper. You will also have a lot of fun along the way, meeting other women and freely giving others the opportunity to take command of their financial futures.

From the functional point of view, in direct sales if you have a well-written compensation plan geared toward the Distributor's benefit, you should be able to make more money from building an organization than from personally selling products. This is true within every MLM plan of which I am aware. The reason it's true is because you are only one person, you only have so many hours of the day to work, and you can only hold so many product Glamour Demos yourself in a given day.

Sponsor others into your business. At Glamour Demos, give attendees the opportunity to become a Distributor. They respond by either saying "yes" or passing for now, which means they "default" to becoming a customer of the product.

The ones who say "yes," become new members or downline Distributors within your sales force, your first-line Distributors who will recreate what

117

you do. They sell products and build their own downlines, and you will receive a commission on all of their sales.

Women who only like conducting Glamour Demos and not sponsoring can still make a good income, but they never realize the true opportunity of a direct-sales MLM compensation plan that also offers residual income for downline commissions.

They'll make enough to buy extra Christmas gifts for the family or take the vacation of their dreams, as long as they are willing to do the work themselves. However, they won't experience a full-fledged career that promises a steady, growing, six-figure income that can support their families for years to come, even when they are no longer conducting Glamour Demos themselves.

There are many SeneGence Independent Distributors who only sell products and do not sponsor others, and some of them are very successful at it. They might sell $100,000 a year. And so their gross profit is 50 percent or $50,000, and even when they subtract their expenses they might still be making 40 percent or $40,000 net profit a year. But they could be doubling or tripling that by developing a downline, and with very little extra effort. Since you are out demo-ing, you are out there potentially sponsoring while you're out there selling, and before you know it your sponsoring-commissions income exceeds your direct-sales income.

Sponsoring is the key that unlocks the door marked "Financial Freedom" in an MLM structure. It's that important. That's why I teach others to develop sponsoring not just as a function, but as an attitude.

I still remember the day Mary Kay Ash took me to task by asking why I wasn't sponsoring more people. "Who died and made you God?" she asked. In that split second the light went on for me. I realized I was making judgments about other people and not offering them the gift to decide for themselves. I was playing God by deciding to whom I would or wouldn't offer this opportunity.

From that day forth I have felt obligated to offer this opportunity to everybody, because, after all, perhaps that's why God landed that person in my path. I don't know in advance who will want to accept this gift of life, of success, of freedom. So I look at every woman as someone who may want this gift, this opportunity. I no longer judge.

At the beginning of each Glamour Demo I say: "Ladies, thank you for coming. By the end of this demo, you will have the opportunity to apply your chosen lip color. At the end of the demo you also will make a choice to become a customer and purchase these products for suggested retail, or you may choose to become a Distributor of these products and purchase them directly through the company at a discount from suggested retail. The choice is yours."

Then we have a great time being girls and applying lip colors and blending and all the things that make a Glamour Demo so much fun.

At the conclusion of the Glamour Demo, following the guidance in the SeneGence Beauty Book and Beauty Book Distributor Guide (which is our comprehensive product guide set), I show everyone the Distributor application in the Beauty Book, talk about options to join me as a Distributor, suggest they complete the application, and we go from there. If they choose to become a customer, I direct them to complete the Customer Purchase Receipt. In the unlikely event they choose to become neither a customer nor a Distributor, I thank them for coming, tell them to please feel free to take our Beauty Book (with my phone number) home, and feel free to call me anytime.

You don't have to be a psychologist to be a successful saleswoman. Simply teach your customers about the products, explain what their options are in using the products, and then stand back and let them make the choices that are best for them. Period. At the very least you have a customer. But what you're looking for are those people who want to become your new distributors, because that's where your real wealth is going to come from. Out of every five women who attend a Glamour Demo, you'll sponsor one new distributor. For every ten, you'll sponsor two.

Having said that, here is my list of what it takes to be successful as a sponsor of new Downline distributors:

1. **Don't prejudge.** Don't decide in advance who will or won't want to take advantage of the opportunity you are offering.

2. **Offer the opportunity to everyone you meet.** Again, you never know who wants (or needs) what you have to offer, regardless of appearances.

3. **Offer the opportunity on an ongoing basis.** If a prospect passes on the opportunity to become a Distributor today, that doesn't mean you can't offer her the opportunity again the next time you meet. You never know what may have changed in her life since your last encounter.

4. **Never push.** Make friends, don't alienate others. They will join your team when they are ready.

5. **Assess needs and offer opportunities.** Be aware that opportunities surround you. The women in your Bunco group might like to start one of their monthly get-togethers with a product Glamour Demonstration. Or, the other women where you work or where your customers work would appreciate an interesting diversion such as a Glamour Demo at lunch one day. Would she like to earn the profits from the Glamour Demo herself as a Distributor, or shall you? Many great Distributors have been born under similar circumstances.

These are five sure-fire ways to share and receive wealth.

❧ Your Turn (Chapter 10) ❧

• **For Direct-Sales professionals: How is your sponsoring going?** Do you actively sponsor new distributors into your organization by sharing all the benefits you are already enjoying in your direct-sales career? Using an easy-to-use computer program such as Microsoft Excel, make a chart of the number of your month-by-month personal sponsoring successes over the last two years (or for as long as you have been building your career in direct sales, up to two years). Now plot your chart out as a line chart. Is the line in your chart going up or going down? Do you even have a line, or is sponsoring something you're waiting on? If so, ask yourself, "Why am I choosing to earn the least possible for my efforts?"

• **Make a list with four columns.** In the first column, write the names of five people who are prospects for you to sponsor as new distributors – people to whom you've never extended the opportunity. Now, in the second column, next to each name, list three reasons why, in your mind, that person will reject the opportunity; In the third column list three reasons why, in your mind, that person will embrace the opportunity. Now, in the fourth column, put a specific date that you intend to ask them again. Make it soon (why not right now? No excuses or self talk allowed!). If you want to remember why you are doing this, go back on the preceding chapter and reread the list of five ways to be successful in sponsoring new distributors.

Chapter 11
The Truth About Direct Sales

I wrote our SeneGence Independent Distributor Compensation Plan to reward our Distributors for helping to build a brand and even more for helping other distributors become successful.

— JONI

Maybe you are reading this book because you are contemplating a career in direct sales as a Distributor. I'd like to offer you a few words of advice on choosing the right direct-sales multilevel marketing company.

One of the things I really love about direct sales is that there is no way to hide in this business. The end result – success or lack of it – is almost always a direct result of your efforts.

If you're doing the actions, focusing on the right activities, you will build a downline and you will build residual income from a direct-sales business. There's no faking it. You reap what you sow. I love that.

There's no other industry where you can jump in and earn money the way that you can in direct sales *if*, in fact, you're willing to do the work. That means wowing, booking demo-ing, directing ... the things we covered in Chapters 9 and 10.

That's the simple truth. So this should be a simple chapter. But it's not quite that easy.

Unlike a job selling this service or that product with a large corporation as part of a dedicated, salary-paid sales force, in direct sales you work for yourself and you have plenty of bosses and colleagues, but in direct sales the catch is that they're all you! As a direct seller, you wear every hat in a company's hat box: CFO, COO,

Sales, Operations, you name it. You do the booking, the planning, handling the finances, you do everything for the business. You are going to become a well-rounded businessperson along the way to becoming successful in direct sales. Once you're successful in direct sales, you can be successful at any business you put your mind to.

First things first: Choose the right direct sales company. How do you decide? There are three important things to keep in mind.

First, you should ... you must ... have a passion for the company's products. If you don't love the product, or you can't even figure out exactly what the company's products are for and what they do to improve a customer's life, move on. If you're not passionate about the company's products, you will be lying when you are wowing and demonstrating the products. Your prospects will sense you are not sincere, which in turn will make your selling and sponsoring efforts less effective. When you are passionate, others see and hear it. Your passion is infectious and helps maximize every effort you make.

Passion puts the "wow" in wowing. Remember, wowing leads to booking, booking leads to demo-ing, and demo-ing leads to Glamour Demo guests becoming either customers of your products or, better yet, new Distributors whom you sponsor on your "first line." Building a downline with distributors on your "first line" is a portion of the $35,000 annual income for each 10 hours a week you work, as discussed in Chapter 9.

So you better believe in the product you represent. You better be passionate about it. Or it will get old fast, and your sales will tank. My motto is, "If you don't love it, don't sell it."

Second, represent a company with a sponsoring focus. Yes you must love the products and love selling those products, but to really build a career you've got to build a downline, as we outlined in the last chapter. So if the company you're thinking about selling for doesn't offer generous returns for helping to build their sales force, then, as they say in New York, "fuggedaboudit."

Third, and most important, look for a company whose compensation

plan doesn't include what is known in the business as "breakage." Breakage is a tricky maneuver; it's an accounting procedure by which most direct sales/multilevel marketing companies reduce your commission on the most successful distributors you sponsor. Breakage increases the company's profits but dramatically *reduces* yours. And that's bad for you.

Direct sales compensation plans that have "breakage" are known as "break away plans." They're easy to find because many of the largest and oldest MLMs have this kind of plan. In fact, years ago it was pretty much the only kind of plan around.

There are other kinds of plans out there, so-called unilevel plans, which reward distributors for having large numbers of direct downlines and continue to compensate you for second-, third-, fourth- and even fifth-level distributors.

Break away and unilevel plans are the most common types of compensation packages in the direct-selling industry.

Other systems out there include "forced matrix" plans and what are known as "binary" plans, but these are less common. A forced matrix plan specifies the number of people you can have on each of a specific number of downline levels. A binary plan is the strangest of all because in it you only have two downline distributors, and you get compensated based on the weaker of the two. Hmmmmmm, I know I want compensation from all downline, weak or not!

There are lots of other models for direct selling companies, and there is plenty of expert and not-so-expert advice on the Web if you search for it. So, make sure you do your homework, especially about "breakage."

In a plan that includes "breakage" a distributor trains and works with a downline to meet a certain sales standard, and when that downline meets that standard she suddenly "breaks away" and becomes her own business entity. So the companies' compensation plan no longer pays the "upline" (that's you!) the same percentages that they were paying to begin with before that distributor and her downline organization "broke away." Once broken away, the company diminishes the payout to the upline. This type of plan is aptly named, because it's a broken idea in my book (literally!).

Here's an example: Suppose you were earning a total of 25 percent combined commission from the sales of a downline organization, because you're earning 10 percent on your direct, or "first-level," downline, 6 percent on their downline, 4 percent on the next level,, 3 percent on the level after that, and 2 percent on the next level again. Now suppose that "first-line" distributor achieves a high level of success and the company "breaks her away" from your downline.

The person you helped to success probably receives a new title, and new bonus and earnings opportunities too. Now instead of 10 percent plus 6 percent plus 4 percent plus 3 percent plus 2 percent commission on that downline's sales you're only getting a maximum of 2 percent, because your downline achieved success.

But you're the one who helped her become successful.

Wow, that hurts!

At SeneGence, our compensation plan has no breakage! So year after year as you build your organization and as they become successful, so too do you! Sponsor and train as many successful Distributors as you choose. We all win!

I wrote our SeneGence Independent Distributor Compensation Plan to reward our Distributors for helping other Distributors become successful. So the earnings of the company are paid to our Distributors at a greater percentage than at most other direct sales/multilevel marketing companies.

Most companies have breakage. We don't. When you're searching for a direct sales MLM opportunity, it pays to understand this accounting and distributor pay practice.

At SeneGence, you earn in direct proportion to what you build. That's a truth you can bank on!

❧ Your Turn (Chapter 11) ❧

• Think about a product you absolutely love. Maybe it's an ice cream flavor, or a parfume or your favorite bathrobe. **Ask yourself, "Could I sell this product to a stranger?"** I'm assuming your answer is "Yes!" Now write down three reasons why a friend should know how great your favorite product is. Include how the product makes you *feel*. Would you enjoy introducing others to something that makes them feel the same way?

• Do an Internet search using your favorite search engine (such as Google) and type in the following search terms (or something similar): "MLM companies with breakage." **Read a few of the articles the search engine finds for you.** While reading make sure you now understand the concept of breakage, and how it figures into a company's compensation plan. Who benefits from breakage?

Chapter 12
Planning to Not Spin Your Wheels (Book to Build)

Those who try our products may choose to become 1) a customer, or 2) a SeneGence Independent Distributor. It doesn't matter which one of these two paths is chosen. SeneGence wants all customers, regardless of which choice they make, to be beautiful, satisfied and prosperous.
— THE SENEGENCE PROMISE

We have a simple, easy-to-understand system at SeneGence that almost guarantees you will be successful as a Distributor — if you follow the system. It's called "Book to Build."

I developed Book to Build based on my personal experiences as a direct-selling representative in the field, plus more than 10 years training and observing the methods of success for thousands of SeneGence Independent Distributors, myself included.

I have seen this approach work over and over again. And I have seen that successful distributors for other companies almost invariably are using their own version of my Book to Build system.

You can be successful in direct sales without applying the principles of Book to Build. But this system, when applied correctly, will significantly enhance any distributor's business growth and overall profits from initial product sales income, reorders and downline commission income earnings. It will help eliminate "spinning your wheels" when building your successful direct-sales career.

Actually, when I teach this system, I call it "Book to Build with BSP." The "BSP" stands for "Basic Sponsoring Principles."

Okay, are you ready for the Book to Build secret? Here it is:

SeneGence offers to each and every person who tries our products the "SeneGence Promise," which is in fact a choice: Those who try our products may choose to become 1) a customer, or 2) a SeneGence Independent Distributor. It doesn't matter which one of these two paths is chosen. SeneGence wants all customers, regardless of which choice they make, to be beautiful, satisfied and prosperous.

That's it – the SeneGence Book to Build business principle of offering every customer a choice. All SeneGence Independent Distributors are taught, from day one, this simple business principle.

Surrounding and supporting this basic principle is the Book to Build system.

Using the principles of Book to Build with BSP, SeneGence Independent Distributors conduct educational and informative demonstrations with the focused intent of identifying and sponsoring new distributors and building a customer base. Every guest attending a SeneGence Glamour Demonstration is given the choice to become a Distributor or a customer, and every follow-up call a SeneGence Independent Distributor makes should do likewise.

By following this simple program, SeneGence Independent Distributors maximize their earnings potential because they are drawing from four distinct income sources:

1. **Income from Immediate Product Sales**

2. **Increased income from Reorders**

3. **Increased Downline Commission income from sponsoring Distributors, and…**

4. **Increased Group Sales Volume bonuses for teaching those Distributors how to build a customer base and their own downlines.**

If you've been working in direct sales for a while, you realize the Book to Build system goes far beyond the simple "party-plan" approach that encourages unstructured get-togethers to simply sell a few products. This is a structured, disciplined approach to business building on four levels. And it works! It really does!

An experienced SeneGence Independent Distributor will tell you product sales are the almost-automatic result of conducting Glamour Demonstrations. In fact, our experience shows 90 percent of the women who attend a SeneGence Glamour Demo will purchase at least one product on the spot, which represents immediate sales income for you. This is a fact that belongs in your business plan.

But guess what? Those immediate, on-the-spot sales at a Glamour Demo also drive a second avenue of income for you: reorders! And by using the basic Book to Build with BSP principle at every Glamour Demo – that is, by offering every customer the choice of becoming a customer or becoming a Distributor – you unlock a third channel of income as well: commission income from "downline" sales, just because they order products directly from the company and upon which you earn commission. And those new Distributors who build a business by selling to others you begin to earn group sales volume bonuses upon qualification.

All four of these revenue channels should be fully appreciated and employed at every Glamour Demonstration. In this all-important hour of your time (the Glamour Demo), if you focus solely on the immediate sales-income opportunity you will inadvertently *minimize* your *overall* profit potential. Who wants to do that?

By sponsoring new Distributors at the very same Glamour Demo, and by following up within two days on any orders with phone calls to your customers to increase sales and gain additional orders (as well as to offer them the chance once again to become a Distributor now that they are really excited about the product results), you will geometrically expand the odds that you reap

SeneGence Distributor
- Earns immediate Sales Income
- Earns future Reorder Income upon those sales
- Books future Demos with attending Guests
- Sponsors new Downline Distributors to earn Downline and Group Sales Volume Bonus Commission Incomes

Guest #1
- Becomes a Customer
- Purchases products: $250
- Books future SeneBlend Demo

At Every Glamour Demo, Each Guest Makes Choices

Guest #5
- Becomes a Distributor
- Purchases products from company
- Books future Launch Demo

Guest #2
- Was the Demo Hostess
- Becomes a Distributor
- Earns products
- Purchases additional products: $200
- Books future Launch Demo

Guest #4
- Becomes a Customer
- Purchases products: $100

Guest #3
- Becomes a Customer
- Purchases products: $150
- Takes Outside Orders from Others to earn payment credit towards product and introduces new customers to Demo Distributor

132

substantially more income from all four channels.

So now you see the importance of this simple point: You "Book to Build" your business by focusing on all four potential income sources at every product demonstration you give. *Voila!*

Later, I'll teach specifically you how to increase the fourth channel, group sales volume bonuses, by helping your Distributors grow their own businesses.

Remember: First you Book. Then you Demo. Then you Direct. It's simple. And it's powerful. Book, Demo, Direct.

Booking means you identify potential future distributors who haven't tried the products. You set a date for a Glamour Demo. And at that demo you let them try the product.

When you demo, you conduct each demo as if you are teaching company and product information to new *Distributors*. This helps them understand better which choice they may want to make, and prepares those who choose to sign up to become *successful* Distributors by showing them from the get-go exactly how the business (particularly Glamour Demos) is done.

You apply the Book to Build principles by helping to direct each attendee into the choice that is right for her: She's either a customer or a Distributor. And you offer a course of action appropriate for each option. You tell those who choose to become Distributors how to purchase products, earn bonus products, partner for profits, host their own launch Glamour Demonstrations and get their new businesses started.

Again, as you are conducting each Glamour Demonstration you are also modeling how to demo for your future downline Distributors, the women at your Glamour Demo who will choose to become Distributors themselves.

Now you know my simple little strategy. Don't be fooled by its simplicity though. By focusing on the three Basic Sponsoring Principles: Book, Demo and Direct, and by offering the SeneGence promise at the beginning and end of every demo — the choice of being a customer or a distributor — and by using these Book to Build principles incessantly, you will be putting into action a time-tested plan for success in direct sales multilevel marketing, even with no training. This alone will help save time and maximize all your potential revenue sources available to you now — without spinning your wheels!

〜 Your Turn (Chapter 12) 〜

• As you have seen in this chapter, there is great opportunity in being able to see the long-range earnings potential of every user of the products. How are you at long-range thinking? Can you identify instances in your own life in which you have failed to see the long-range opportunity present in a job, or in a relationship or maybe even in an opportunity to serve others at church or in your community? Sometimes it is hard to see how the choices we make now can pay dividends far into the future; dividends of which we were not even aware at the time. Spend a few minutes making your own list of long-range opportunities in your life today. Start with your career in direct sales or wherever you work. Can you see now how there may be hidden benefits for the future in what you do?

Chapter 13
Achieving Goals with Basic Work Principles

Joni has always had this dream of starting a company that would empower women. She had the vision early on to create that kind of business model. All she needed was the right product. And ultimately that fell into place as well ... It isn't surprising, really. When you know what you want to accomplish , and you have discipline, things just start to happen.

— JERRY HIGHT, Joni's Stepfather ("Dad Jerry")

In the previous chapters we discussed the basics of developing a successful direct sales/multilevel marketing business career. Now let's talk about the habits that you must develop to support your business plan.

Good work habits are the key that will open the door to success. And if you haven't already done so, now is the time to start developing and implementing them.

I've often heard others call direct sales "a personal growth course in which you are paid while growing." There's a lot of truth in that statement, because direct sales requires you to grow as a human being and constantly analyze your motivation, perceptions, realities and self-image.

You will change and grow as a person in direct proportion to the extent that you change and grow as a direct-sales professional. This is not a career for the person who doesn't want to change. It takes a lifelong effort to extend, re-evaluate and reorganize yourself as you prosper from one level of growth to the next in direct sales. The more "self-help" you engage in and implement, the more rewards you will reap.

What a great deal: The more we know and grow, the more results we show!

So, get ready to change for the better. A great place to start is by internalizing my Basic Work Principles. I developed this simple checklist of rules or, if you prefer, habits that will propel your success forward ... no matter where you begin.

Once you master these principles, they will also help you enrich any other areas of your life you desire to improve. Successfully applied and practiced, the principles will be passed along to your family and friends, enriching their lives as well, simply because you are "modeling" these success practices on a daily basis.

The Basic Work Principles are:

1. Get Out of Your Own Way.

2. Do the Work.

3. Follow Through.

Basic Work Principle #1: Get Out of Your Own Way!

This is one of the toughest assignments you must master. Remember, your success in direct sales is going to be based on your ability to help others, offering excellent products and a great opportunity to everyone you meet. To help others, to offer assistance and guidance to a new downline Distributor or a customer, you must avoid "pre-judging" and learn to ask and listen.

Do not assume to know what others know – *Ask* others what they know. Do not assume to know what others think – *Ask* them what they think. Do not assume to know what others want – *Ask* them what they want. Do not assume to know what others expect – *Ask* others what they expect. Do not assume to know what others feel – *Ask* what they feel.

Develop an *attitude* of asking. Sounds easy? Then why do so few practice it?

The "attitude of asking" means you never put your "stuff" on someone else. Others have different opinions than yours; Learn what they think. Others have different life experiences and realities from yours; Learn their realities. Others are motivated by different circumstances and opportunities than those that motivate you; Learn what motivates others.

In my home office hang two paintings that illustrate this principle beautifully. One day, soon after becoming a single mother, I invited a girlfriend, Lady Kala Brunick, to my home. Kala is an accomplished artist.

She offered to give me a few "painting" tips while visiting, and she happened to have canvases and paint in her car, so we decided to both paint a flower arrangement that was sitting on a table in my home. Each of us spent the afternoon painting the same vase of flowers onto our own canvas, but the outcome was amazingly different!

We were both looking at the same object, but our interpretations of the object were not at all the same! I keep these paintings hanging in my office to remind me of this principle every day, reminding me that no two people see the world in the same way. So if indeed you want to better communicate, better understand, better support, ask how you can best serve the other person. Try to see it from her perspective.

Focus on others, on those you meet while wowing and demo-ing and those you meet at social gatherings and parties, at church, everywhere. Focus on them, not on yourself.

Educate them and then step away. Let them make educated decisions for themselves.

Step away after guiding them. Let them choose the path they will travel.

Step away after offering choices to them. Let them make their own decisions based upon choices that best suit their own needs.

Step away after offering them support. Let them determine what type and how much support they require.

In other words, by practicing the first Basic Work Principle, Get Out of Your Own Way, you are shifting the focus away from controlling others and their responses, and learning how to offer help without demanding a particular response. Let others choose their own paths, based on the choices you provide.

Basic Work Principle #2: Do the Work! Ah, here is where a basic work ethic comes into the picture. It is often said in direct sales that "You get what you work for. Nothing more. Nothing less." Isn't that a wonderful and objective reality?

In direct sales, the results of your labors in sales and sponsoring success are measured by the value of sales income and commission-income earnings. And those results belong to you and you alone.

Here's the good news: You can learn a good work ethic. Even if you don't already have a good work ethic, the business of direct selling will give you the opportunity and the time to develop a great work ethic of your own, while developing a sound and profitable business.

But you must "do the work." You must create a plan and work the plan. Part of this discipline is being accountable to yourself. Your goals and objectives are yours. You must own them and be willing to "do the work" to achieve them.

Basic Work Principle #3: Follow Through! The results you want will manifest when you learn to follow through in the entire selling process, which yields increased sales and sponsoring. If you don't follow through, you will see greatly reduced results. Practice makes perfect, no matter what.

No matter how you feel, even if you are afraid of rejection, you will soon find grace through practice in allowing others to follow their own paths. If you feel inferior to others, you will soon become secure in your success and uplifted by your acumen, just because results become significant when you follow through. If you lack confidence, your consistent effort and experiences in direct sales will build your confidence in yourself, your abilities and your progress. And if you don't know what to do or where to begin, direct sales will be your perfect training ground, as you will receive support from your upline and the company.

Ask and tell – Ask questions and learn, then tell others about the extraordinary products and opportunity you have to share. Ask and tell even if someone seems to have it all: money, home, looks, great job and fabulous personality. Ask and tell even when you determine they are indifferent, defiant, snobbish, scattered, busy, lofty, professional, curious or even interested (imagine that!). No matter what your first impression of someone is, ask and tell.

Finally, no matter what others say, engage them in the possibilities of a SeneGence career. Offer each the opportunity to choose for herself, despite what anyone else may have told you about that person's interest or lack of it. Do this no matter what anyone else's opinion is of this business. Just follow through with your "ask and tell," offer-the-choice approach and see if I'm right. I am!

These are ideas they never taught us in formal school settings and institutions. If schools taught this, we would already know how to do the "successful entrepreneur independent distributor thing."

One of the reasons why people fail in networking businesses such as direct selling is that they are emotionally unprepared to sustain their efforts in an atmosphere of constant potential rejection. They are not mentally tough enough to endure the necessary emotional growth that precedes success in a commission-based profession like network marketing. The emotional turmoil experienced as a result of analysis on many levels created by this profession can eat you up and spit you out, unless you're prepared with these Basic Work Principles, and you realize you've become one of the few adults who voluntarily enter a stage of perpetual change and growth, learning and improvement. That path ultimately will bring the "journey person" great joys never yet experienced!

According to Networking Times, only about 10 percent of us last and thrive in direct sales.

The real reason some fail as independent distributors is that their lack of knowledge precludes them from progressing. They begin the journey but don't know how to invest the proper time and energy to grow into successively higher levels of achievement. They get distracted. Old habits take over. Or they get frustrated because growth is a workout for your brain, heart and muscles.

So, now you know your success will require stretching, flexing, redefining, reevaluating, trial and error, studying, practice and more. No more excuses. Get educated and improve yourself and join the 10 percent of us who succeed! I know you can.

These Basic Work Principles will help you get there.

Remember in Chapter 2 I talked about Napoleon Hill and his book *Think and Grow Rich*? Have you read that book? If not, I suggest you get yourself to a bookstore right now and buy a copy.

Hill describes "13 **Characteristics of Successful People**," and you should begin today in the effort to make these traits your own. They include:

1. Desire
2. Faith
3. Auto Suggestion
4. Specialized Knowledge
5. Imagination
6. Organized Planning
7. Decision
8. Persistence

9. Master Mind
10. Enthusiasm
11. Subconscious Mind
12. The Brain
13. The Sixth Sense

Get Hill's book and learn what each of these 13 characteristics mean to you. Mastering them will change your life.

Meanwhile, while you are learning to master the Basic Work Principles and Napoleon Hill's Characteristics of Successful People, focus on mustering up some faith in yourself and in the guiding hand of your Creator. After all, you are one of the few stepping up to improve and achieve.

If, at this point, you do not have faith in yourself and your abilities, have faith in an ultimate outcome for building and mastering each of Napoleon Hill's success characteristics. Mastering the characteristics will, in turn, build faith in yourself.

And remember: No effort will stand unless built upon Absolute Truth.

I seek these characteristics in my prayers. Every night I pray for "Courage, Wisdom, and a Strength of Heart and Mind."

There are also other characteristics I seek. I will share them with you and I encourage you to consider them:

Seek to be a "visionary" so that you might not limit progress through shortsightedness, making decisions for immediate results that may not support longevity in business and in life.

Seek spiritual enlightenment and divine guidance so that you may live in passion and spend life performing to the best of your limited (but growing) abilities. Apply this intent to each and every role in life and in business, because each role blends into another.

Seek physical, mental and emotional strength so that you may maintain endurance to consistently progress while experiencing as much of the natural beauty of this world as possible.

Seek the courage to walk through each and every door that has been opened for you – to step through, although you may be afraid and know you lack skill, experience and knowledge.

Seek clarity that helps you understand the complexities of human behaviors and cultures, the human condition and overall standards and expectations that all humanity, regardless of demographics, race, age, education or social position, should be held to uphold personally and collectively.

Seek to learn forgiveness so that you might first forgive yourself for your own failures and faults; and ask others to forgive you as you forgive them.

Seek to know first each person's heart looking for the love and for the goodness in every living being.

Strive to find the humor and silver lining in every situation.

Building upon truth and using Basic Work Principles makes achieving goals simple.

There is one publication that has most helped to provide answers, solutions and guidance for me in my quest for "Wisdom, Courage and Strength of Heart and Mind": *The Holy Bible*.

I highly recommend it.

❧ Your Turn (Chapter 13) ❧

• After reading this chapter can you see where you get in your own way? Name all of the ways you get in your own way.

• Are you ready to apply the Basic Work Principles on a daily basis? Here's your chance to get started. Are you trying to unnecessarily control the outcome of others' decisions? Get out a blank sheet of paper. Now, on the left-hand side of the sheet write the following words: 1) Customers, co-workers, 2) Children, 3) Other family members (including parents), 4) Friends, 5) Neighbors, and 6) Others. For each of these six categories, see if you can name at least three situations in which you are "holding on." Remember, your role is to offer others guidance, choices and support. Beyond that, you have to let others follow their own paths. So, why not get to work right now identifying these opportunities for you to "let go?" I'll bet if you're like me when you first begin this practice you may find you can fill the entire sheet of paper in no time.

• Take another look at Napoleon Hill's 13 Characteristics of Successful People in this chapter. Which of them do you feel you've made progress on in your life so far? Write them down. And which do you feel are most lacking, or make no sense to you at all? Write them down too. Now go to your local bookstore or local library and get a copy of Hill's *Think and Grow Rich*. Read it today and watch your life change!

∽ Your Turn (Chapter 13 cont'd) ∽

• Pray this simple prayer at least twice a day for the next week: "Lord, give me courage, wisdom and strength of heart and mind to do your bidding. Amen." Try making it your final thought of the day after you close your eyes to sleep. See if it makes a difference in your life. It did in mine.

Chapter 14
Nothing Happens Until the Selling Starts

If you are already using SeneGence products, at some point you are going to have to believe in the products and in the confidence we give women. One day you will look at an old picture of yourself, taken prior to using SeneDerm Skincare, and you will see startling improvement in your own skin since you started using SeneGence. I guarantee it.

— JONI

Throughout this book we've been talking about direct sales and the direct-selling environment. In this chapter I would like to put some emphasis on the *"sales"* part of "direct sales."

Without a sale, there is nothing, *absolutely nothing* that is going to happen for you in this career path. You can show products to friends at demos and be a master planner and read training materials and attend networking events until, as they say, the cows come home. But nothing, absolutely nothing, is going to earn income until you begin selling something.

In direct sales, selling is the foundation for everything.

There are two important parts to selling: The first part is about you and how you present yourself and your products, and the second is about the products or opportunities themselves.

The selling relationship begins the very first moment you meet somebody. That initial meeting forms a perception in the mind of a customer; of who you are as an individual and how you can be of service to her or him. Your tone of voice, your attitude, your physical presence, your cleanliness, your attractiveness – these all play into how you are perceived. It's everything about you.

Not only do you begin the sales relationship by first selling yourself, but you also lay the groundwork for a valuable relationship and you build trust while this is happening. You are always on stage in this "show" of selling, wherever you go and whatever you do. You might be casually walking through an aisle of flowers at the supermarket and someone sees you and perceives who and what you are by the way you are smelling the flowers and making a selection. You are always on stage. You are always demonstrating who you are to others around you in your life.

Selling *is* a way of life.

Pay close attention to the details of your life. Start at home, and start with how you prepare for your day.

Every time you walk out the front door you should look the part of a successful saleswoman: clean and well put together. Wear SeneGence cosmetics. And, like Napoleon Hill suggested, have your pleasing personality on, so that you can attract and retain the interest of others.

I suppose this process is made easier if you are born with natural good looks and good taste, and you have the wherewithal to dress yourself well and apply color cosmetics. But who would know all of this intuitively?

I wasn't born into a family of material wealth so I had to learn how to develop the qualities I sought over time and how to make the most of my appearance without spending a lot of money. I learned that beauty comes from something much deeper than looking like a model and spending lots of money on the latest cosmetics trend or gimmick.

Simple beauty is best. Grandmother Rogers, for one, was an early example to me of how to look beautiful by always trying to look your best, even at home.

The strongest example of simple beauty, simple refinement, to me is Maureen Dean, the wife of John Dean, one of the Watergate defendants and former White House Counsel under U.S. President

Richard Nixon.

Maureen Dean was always graceful and composed and beautiful during those long Watergate hearings on television, which I watched every day as a young and impressionable adult in 1973.

Dean always wore her blond hair pulled neatly back, and wore pearls in her ears every day of the hearings. She just exuded confidence, and I was mesmerized by her stoic beauty.

I vividly remember how she stood out in her red and yellow suits in a sea of grey flannel. As her husband struggled on the witness stand, she sat composed, strong, beautiful and elegant.

I thought, "Wow, is she beautiful!" Her skin appeared flawless, her makeup was beautiful, she was clean and crisp-looking every single day, She was just stunning. Honestly, I wasn't looking at her physical features. Instead, it was the way she put herself together that made the "package." That was and is to me a model of true attractiveness. I would have bought anything she was selling!

So the sales process definitely begins with us, with the way we present ourselves to customers and prospects in the marketplace.

If Part One of sales is how we present ourselves, Part Two of sales is about the products and opportunities we present to customers.

I've heard people say a good salesperson can sell anything to anybody. I have no idea if that's true, but I truly believe that a good salesperson wouldn't be motivated to sell someone something they don't really want or don't really need. Why would they?

If a product isn't right for you, a good salesperson will say so. The good salesperson finds a way for everyone to win. It's not about making money (though that's an objective), it's about helping others. I'll cover more of this in Chapter 19, The Art of Selling.

Of course, sales technique is important too. But, for example, selling SeneGence SenseCosmetics and SeneDerm Skincare isn't the result of using a lot of fancy psychology or memorizing sales scripts or whatever. What it is about is learning to eliminate personal barriers and limitations that might prevent you from wanting to share these incredible products with another woman. You are driven to share just because it's the right thing to do. You have an incredible gift, and your responsibility is to pass it on!

You pass it on by engaging other women in gracious conversations. The more often you do this, the easier it becomes. Practice makes perfect when it comes to building new relationships by starting conversations that will eventually open the sales door to prosperity.

I bet I've started more than 5,000 conversations about cosmetics with women in the past 20 years. It takes hundreds, if not thousands, of "started" conversations to really get the hang of initiating them. So keep practicing. It gets easier.

It should be easy to tell another women: "Try this fantastic product, which you are going to fall in love with and which is going to resolve a lot of small irritations in your life. It's going to resolve mussiness, sweatiness, feelings of inadequacy. You will have better days because you will no longer be worried about what used to be necessary primping. And by using our products you are actually making your skin more beautiful! You're applying products onto your skin that are not going to harm you, they are going to make your skin *more radiant, moister, firmer, and all the while reducing fine lines and wrinkles.*

"First try the products and you can choose to pay suggested retail as my customer, or you may choose to pay wholesale by becoming a Distributor of the product."

There's that SeneGence Promise again. Remember the last chapter?

I open conversations like this and I believe that I am convincing and natural because I absolutely believe in what I am saying.

If you don't fully believe this at the beginning of your career as a

SeneGence Independent Distributor, you will eventually believe it. You will see what a gift you have to present to others.

When you use the products, at some point you will have to believe in them because you will look at an old picture of yourself and you see the improvements in your own skin using SeneGence SenseCosmetics and SeneDerm Skincare. There is no comparison. And at some point there can be no question in your mind that you are offering women a gift by presenting SeneGence products. Women agree their skin definitely becomes more beautiful as they progress in this business.

"If you don't believe in yourself, believe in the process," said Napoleon Hill.

Samuel Johnson, a friend of the founders of the revered Anchor Brewery in 18th Century London, gave a classic sales talk more than 200 years ago that is still inspirational today. He was speaking at the sale of the brewery to new owners who would soon turn it into the largest in the world.

"We are not here to sell a parcel of boilers and vats," said Johnson, "but the potentiality of growing rich beyond the dreams of avarice." Johnson wasn't just talking about ale, I think he was talking about the viewpoint of the successful saleswoman or salesman. He was talking about looking beyond the mere products and prices and seeing something more important at stake in business. He was talking about seeing the opportunities of the future.

He recognized pure "potentiality" – the same "pure potentiality" that I see in every new SeneGence Independent Distributor.

"Nothing happens until somebody sells something!" I've never forgotten that in order to put food on our table, we must first sell.

And selling begins with "booking." Remember our lessons from the last few chapters? If you need to do so, go back and review them now.

Here's a typical SeneGence sales scenario:

Imagine "Susie," an enthusiastic new SeneGence Independent Distributor, who meets her new friend Sally for lunch at the food court. Susie applied Red Cherry lip color to her own lips and onto the back of her hand before she left the house. Sally spies the color on Susie's hand and curiously inquires.

"Looks like you forgot to clean those color samples off your hand," Sally says, smiling.

Susie smiles back.

"Actually, it's kind of tough to get these samples to come off," Susie says. "These are LipSense long-lasting lip colors, and earlier I was trying to figure out which color would be just right for today. But here's the proof that they really work: I can't rub them off! Let's book a demonstration together sometime in the near future so you can try these products yourself!"

Sally agrees, and they book a date, time and place.

What are the likely outcomes of the Glamour Demonstration that takes place as a result of this booking? Susie will successfully conduct the demonstration on the appointed date and time with Sally and a handful of her friends. Susie will earn profits from immediate sales ($50? $150? $500?), and she will add new customers she had not met prior to this event, Sally's girlfriends, to her reorder customer service base.

But despite this apparent success, Susie left money on the table. She missed the chance to maximize her new-business development returns because she offered Sally only half the choice available to every woman who tries SeneGence SenseCosmetics and SeneDerm Skincare.

The point at which Susie offered – at too early a moment – to conduct the Glamour Demonstration for Sally and her friends was the point of lost opportunity. That's because Susie offered Sally only the opportunity to try the products and did not extend to

Sally the offer to consider earning income by selling the products herself. And then to compound the lost opportunity, she did not extend the choice to Sally's friends, either.

Ouch.

How could this scenario have gone if Susie were truly understanding and appreciative of the new business development opportunity available to her?

Let's try it again ...

Susie, an enthusiastic new SeneGence Independent Distributor, meets her new friend Sally for lunch at the food court. Susie applied Red Cherry lip color to her own lips and onto the back of her hand before she left the house. Sally spies the color on Susie's hand and curiously inquires.

"Looks like you forgot to clean those color samples off your hand," Sally says, smiling.

Susie smiles back.

"Actually, it's kind of tough to get them to come off," Susie says. "These are LipSense long-lasting lip colors and I was trying to figure out which color would be just right for today. But here's the proof they really work: I can't rub them off! Let's book a Glamour Demonstration together sometime in the near future so you can try these products yourself!

"You know," Susie continues, "once you try these products you may choose to become either a customer of these products and pay retail or you may choose to become a Distributor like me and pay wholesale. Either way, you are going to love these products!"

Sally is excited. Together they agree upon a date, time and place for the Glamour Demonstration.

What are the probable results this time around? Susie will successfully conduct a Glamour Demonstration with Sally and her friends, extending the SeneGence promise (the choice to become a customer or a Distributor) to Sally and each guest. Susie will earn profits from immediate sales and add new customers to her reorder customer service base. She will also identify those guests who are considering the opportunity to become a new SeneGence Independent Distributor. She will "direct" by following up with each accordingly, with both customers and new potential Distributors, booking future Glamour Demos and signing up her new downline Distributors.

Congratulations, Susie. You've come to understand that, in direct sales, selling is more than just the sale alone. It's also recognizing that every selling situation is an opportunity to build commissions by sponsoring new Distributors. By using this simple yet powerful principle, Susie could be on her way to earning a great income by working 20 hours a week.

If you're not already achieving a substantial income in direct sales and you've read this far into this book, let me ask you: *Hasn't the time come for you to begin selling products that really work and realizing the unique opportunity that SeneGence offers?* Join us in taking the next step.

≋ Your Turn (Chapter 14) ≋

• Write a short list of five women who are beautiful to you. Go beyond simple "runway" beauty and include women on your list who exhibit a deeper beauty you recognize in their poise, charm or courage. After each name on your list, write two or three adjectives that describe what it is about each that makes her beautiful to you. Are you surprised by any of the women on your list? Now add to your list: Can you name the first woman in your life whom you remember as beautiful? What was it about her that struck you as being so beautiful?

• Have you ever bought something that changed your life? Something that wasn't apparent to you until a salesperson recognized an opportunity to offer you a life-changing product that could truly enhance your life? Maybe it was your first exposure to SeneGence LipSense. Or a line of apparel that has become exactly "your style." Or maybe it was a book that changed the way you think. Do you see now what a positive effect the willingness to share and sell (or sponsor) something can have on another's life?

Chapter 15
Get Off Your Laurels

I thought of Joni yesterday and a valuable lesson that I learned from her. We were having lunch before a business meeting and she received some difficult personal news. She finished the phone call and continued lunch as though nothing was wrong. I was amazed! I stopped our conversation and asked "HOW can you do that? You must feel very sad." Joni replied, "I WILL deal with the emotions later. But people are depending on me now. The show must go on."

Now I sit by my 49-year-old sister's bedside, nursing her during the final days of her fight with ovarian cancer. There are times I am tempted to just collapse and let the emotions take over. Then I remember Joni's words and I know the show must go on. People are depending on me! And I WILL have time to tend to my emotions later. Thanks to you Joni, I have learned a balance that is invaluable to me. I'm forever grateful.

— LEANNE AVANT, SeneGence Independent Distributor (Crown Princess)

I speak often to independent distributors at SeneGence about "getting off your laurels."

I'm certain you've heard the phrase "resting on your laurels," which means relying on past achievements instead of working for your own progress in life and business. The person who is resting on her laurels has a hard time advancing in life, and instead is always looking to the past and resting there instead of in the moment or in the future.

So "getting off your laurels" is about not resting on your laurels. It's about making a decision instead to choose to move forward, now.

I have witnessed women in direct sales – men too – who have a huge challenge in taking that first step and putting one foot ahead of another to begin a project such as embarking on a direct-sales career. Direct sales demands self-motivation. But how do you create that motivation to get dressed in the morning, and make a turn in the right direction to make progress each and every day?

That can be a huge challenge, and for me it's a challenge I face every morning. It really is.

Virtually every single day upon waking my mind tries to talk me out of what I'm supposed to do that day. And if I allowed my mind to actually do that, I know it would directly affect the end result of what my life will look like 10 years from now.

So how do you deal with that issue? More specifically, how do you better manage time within every day, knowing ultimately that the accumulation of each of these days and how you spend those hours will determine the outcome of what life – for you and your family – looks like in 20 years? Answer: Follow a well-thought-out plan of action designed to keep moving you forward.

When you're an independent business owner, you *are* the business and you don't have to be at the office every day at eight o'clock because you're the boss who makes the rules. It can be a challenge to stay motivated on a daily basis. But you've got to do it; You've got to get off your laurels.

Getting off your laurels comes down to knowing your own self, knowing where your strengths and weaknesses are. Knowing your strengths and weaknesses allows you to schedule accountability points into your daily schedule so that you are forced to stay on task.

Here's my advice: Make appropriate appointments, lots of them.

Pre-scheduled appointments are accountability points. As a direct-sales professional (which is what you are or probably want to be or you wouldn't have already read this far into this book), "getting off your laurels" is probably your toughest daily challenge. Focused appointments can play a key role in helping to propel you, even force you, into success.

Face it. You wear many hats. You have to set aside various periods of time during the week to complete the many and varied tasks before you, but you have to do it in a way that builds balance in your life so you can consistently achieve progress in many areas. To do this, you must compartmentalize your life (see Page 76).

Consider the many tasks the majority of women face daily: A house to maintain, jobs, family members to care for and love, and the fact that each of these responsibilities is distinct and in many way separate from the others. Now add to the mix: A business to build through wowing and booking and demo-ing, bills to pay, other financial responsibilities, social responsibilities, spiritual responsibilities and so on.

These responsibilities are all part of what I and others call "The Life Balance Wheel." You need to take care of all the areas of your Life Balance Wheel or the "wheel" goes flat and soon it becomes a pretty bumpy ride on your out-of-kilter wheel of life. For more details on The Life Balance Wheel, see Chapter 21.

Get to know yourself. Know where your own strengths and weaknesses are. Then set out to build accountability in any areas in which progress or growth are an issue.

For me, the accountability process includes using my date book and pre-scheduling my activities, including everything from a date night with my husband to individual lunches with my children and social lunches with girlfriends.

Schedule everything you can: Set aside two three-hour blocks a week to conduct Glamour Demos, one period of two hours a week to organize and clean up your office and take care of other work-related tasks. Of course you also set aside time to do all those other things like caring for your house, yard, automobiles, social activities, church activities and so on.

Take a look at each of those categories. Make commitments with other people in your datebook, and resolve to follow through on that commitment. That's "getting off your laurels!"

Plan for success. I like the popular saying: "Plan your work and work your plan." It's absolutely true.

Dad Jerry once reminded me, as I was about to speak to a large group, that a person without a plan to follow is like a ship without a course. You've got no place to go, and disaster is a probability.

Making a decision is the opposite of procrastination. I've learned that those who can't make decisions well make them slowly and change them often. I've also learned that opinions are the cheapest of commodities, and it's unwise to let others sway our decisions with their opinions.

In business, as in life, you choose a destination, chart a course and set sail on your life journey. It's that simple. Appropriate pre-scheduled appointments help you stay on course.

A common reason for failure in direct sales is the inability to get off your laurels. It can also be called "procrastination."

The Bible says, in Proverbs 6:6-11:
Take a lesson from the ants, you lazybones.
Learn from their ways and become wise!
Though they have no prince or governor or ruler to make them work,
They labor hard all summer, gathering food for the winter.
But you, lazybones, how long will you sleep?
When will you wake up?
A little extra sleep, a little more slumber, a little folding of the hands to rest —
Then poverty will pounce on you like a bandit; scarcity will attack you

like an armed robber."
(New Living Translation)

In other words, "Get up and get to work!" Words to live by. "Getting off your laurels" means learning this lesson from the Bible about the lowly ant. Choose to model the ant! That's what it takes to be successful in direct sales.

Direct sales is for people who want to take control and be in charge of their destiny.

If living day by day as it unfolds, with no real intention at work in your life, seems okay, then maybe direct sales is not for you. But if you want a way to make dreams happen, maybe you belong in direct sales.

Joni's Rule #1: Be beholden to others. Being beholden to others means you are counting on others and your life is based on your commitments to others. You work a schedule that includes all of the important functions in your life: family, home, spiritual, education, financial, career, health. Schedule time for each category. Plan events and appointments with other people whom you are beholden to and are also working toward the same end, within each category. Do it each and every week of the year, keep your word and commitments and you will make tremendous progress toward your goals.

Joni's Rule #2: See Rule #1. There is no other important thing. Don't allow yourself to talk yourself out of progress. Keep your word. Attend and give 100 percent of yourself to the intention of the appointments. Be beholden to others.

Mary Kay Ash was dogmatic about getting up early every day and being productive and accountable. She rarely wasted even an hour. She changed the way women live today as a result of that effort.

Business Coach Anthony Robbins is another model of "getting

off your laurels." Tony has come from having very little to being a self-made billionaire. Today he's known as one of the greatest business minds alive.

I've attended workshops with him, even walked on hot coals with him, and I've never met anybody quite as passionate as Tony when he's advocating taking the reins on how you choose to live every hour of every day. It's your choice.

Tony's mentor was a man named Jim Rohn, who helped Tony see early in life that we are who we become in life not so much because of what we have, but because of how we choose to live. When Rohn was only 25 he was already in debt and trying to figure out a better way in life. And he was a millionaire by 31. That's what results from getting off your laurels and getting into gear.

There's powerful synergy between Rohn, Robbins and others who have influenced me, such as Napoleon Hill, Norman Vincent Peale and Mary Kay Ash.

Tony Robbins takes these ideas further, exploring how food choices, proper breathing and other choices regarding our bodies also make us who we are. Tony is a big proponent of neuro-linguistic programming, which is a very fancy way of saying we can overcome what we think are our limitations by working with positive approaches to thinking and living. I'm all for it.

Remember what I said earlier in this book? My mantra is "choose to live life in love and abundance, and then work for it." That's what "getting off your laurels" means.

Stop pretending like you don't know any better! When you have an idea and you know you have the ability to do something about it and you don't do it, I think that's a crime against nature, a sin against God.

You are given information, abilities and strengths to get something done on this planet, and if you do not do it, you are falling short of why you were set here on Earth. I believe to be content and fulfilled you must fulfill your mission. You have an obligation to do exactly that.

If you catch yourself not striving for anything in particular and achieving far less than you are capable of, just demand of yourself, "Stop pretending like I don't know I can do something spectacular with my life." Say it nicely, but say it.

I believe people must motivate themselves. I know that the motivation within me comes from a selfish place in that I am motivated to "produce" for my sons. I know I have a certain lifespan and I'd better do what I can each day toward building this company, developing my family and helping others, because when I am gone, that's it.

I want to have confidence that in those final seconds of my life I will know that my children will be well cared for, that they will have security. If that's coming from a selfish place, well, that's okay with me because this effort (and that of our Distributors) helps a whole lot of people along the way.

I don't allow laziness within my character. I've got all these thoughts and ideas running around in my mind about what a good wife is, what a good mother is, and what makes a good mentor, friend, sister, daughter and businesswoman. I have a specific mission to deliver products that really work at a price the majority of the women in the world can truly afford. And so on. These are the things that really matter to me in life and business.

Remember back in Chapter 8 we talked about writing down your Real Goal or Goals and putting them in your wallet? Here's a tip to help you get off your laurels: Go back and reread that Real Goal or those Goals frequently. Doing so will help you refresh your focus and attention and stay on the positive course – the path you set to attain your goals.

Finally, discover your burning desires. Determine how your ongoing efforts will be dedicated and what that outcome will look like in each area of your life. Once identified, I believe you will be self-motivated to follow your path and to fulfill your destiny. You will have no choice but to "get off your laurels."

Your Turn (Chapter 15)

• Do you feel that you "choose to live life in love and abundance, and then work for it?" Be honest.

• Are you beholden to others? If not, why not? Make a list of all of the people and areas of your life that are important to you today – your family, your home, your church or spiritual life, education, finances, health and fitness, and so on. Consider how much time you spent during the past seven days engaged in/working on each. Estimate, try to come within a few hours. Count up the hours for each category and order the list starting with those categories on which you spent the most time, and moving to those categories your spent the least amount of time on. Does the list reflect your priorities?

Chapter 16
Becoming a SeneGence Savior (The Gift of Giving)

My children and I shared our home and resources with Joni and Alan, giving them the financial and emotional support needed during their difficult times. Even then, Joni shared with me her dream of starting a company that would empower women to be independent and successful and to allow them the security and ability to provide for their families and loved ones.

— CARMEN HOLLADAY

Becoming a SeneGence Savior is really all about receiving and sharing a precious gift.

As a SeneGence Independent Distributor you represent a product line that really does work. You help women resolve skin-care problems and maybe even self-esteem problems that used to afflict them. You've already received the gift of excellent products that create beautiful skin, and you've also received the gift of the opportunity to become a Distributor.

As a result, you help other women feel better about themselves and their lives as you share this gift with them. Truly, this is an act of kindness, often random, that you received and can now pay forward.

As a Distributor, each time you introduce these powerful products to a woman, you are actually helping to improve this world in which we live on a daily basis through random acts of kindness.

I love that phrase, "Practice random acts of kindness." It came from a writer named Anne Herbert who lives in Northern California, and you probably know that it's grown into a very popular movement. It's something I believe in and practice.

I still remember the many random acts of kindness extended to me by Dorothy Zumwalt, the mother of my childhood friend in Sapulpa, Oklahoma. What an impact Mrs. Zumwalt had on my life! She taught me early in life that giving is the greatest blessing of all. Giving is the key to life and to love.

Today when children of my friends, or friends of my sons, Alan and William, walk through our front door I go out of my way to create opportunities to practice random acts of kindness and engage the children in experiences of kindness.

When I think about random acts of kindness I also think about Delia Semthop, the mother of Alan's lifelong friend Daniel.

I owe a thank-you note to Delia, because she has had a huge impact on my son's life through the many random acts of kindness she has extended to Alan over the years. Delia is a holistic physician, and her words of wisdom have made my son a healthier person than he would have been without her in his life. Today, Alan cares about excellent health and great nutrition. His happiness in this area is largely a result of the many gifts Delia has shared with him over the years.

I can only hope that on a personal level I am able to pass along to others what Delia has given so freely to me – the gift of sharing and caring for others and extending random acts of kindness to others.

I also feel fortunate just to be involved with SeneGence Skincare products. Almost daily I see women feel better about themselves through the use of our products – and that also includes me! My skin is better today than it was 20 and 30 years ago. SeneGence Skincare makes me feel better in so many ways, and as a result of feeling that way I know I am a more loving mother, a more thoughtful wife, and hopefully I am a more gracious person with whom to work and socialize.

Think about what this product does for the woman who

chooses to become a Distributor. For example, just look at SeneGence Crown Princess Sheila Young, one of the top Distributors at SeneGence year after year and serving as one of California's State Founders. Recently, Sheila completely gutted and redecorated her house with the money she has made selling SeneGence SenseCosmetics and SeneDerm Skincare. She has been blessed to travel with her children to places around the world, participating in SeneGence incentive trips she has earned. Before she became a Distributor, Sheila had never gone on a cruise with her husband. Now she takes him with her to Australia, The Caribbean, Hawaii, you name it.

I know SeneGence women who, unfortunately, like me, have gone through divorces, but still supported themselves and their children with their SeneGence earnings while gaining the freedom and flexibility to "be there" for their children. That's a real gift.

Leta Greene, a SeneGence Independent Distributor (Royal) supported her family while her husband was recuperating in the hospital after being run over by a city bus! Here is a perfect model of composure under fire. She had already put him through law school on her SeneGence income. Today, her husband has recovered, has a job as an attorney, and they are enjoying their beautiful life together, blessed with two active children as she continues to build her SeneGence business as Utah's State Leader.

When you represent products that really work, and benefit from an unequalled opportunity and compensation plan that works, expect to hear lots of similar stories. I call these women "SeneGence Saviors," which is what they are to so many others within their communities. And, in turn, these SeneGence Saviors reap immense rewards for themselves and their families.

The idea behind being a SeneGence Savior is to be more than simply financially successful. It's about realizing that you can do good in the world while also living well. Since I know what I have to offer is ultimately going to help someone, this knowledge alone serves as a huge motivator for me. Helping others by serving their needs is what makes someone a SeneGence Savior, in my estimation.

SeneGence Independent Distributors have an opportunity to help every single woman, to make her skin more beautiful and present her with the opportunity to be financially free, strong and secure. In a sense, SeneGence Independent Distributors can just stand back after demo-ing the product line and let their customers decide whether they are going to use the products to make them more confident, to have beautiful skin, or choose even more by becoming Distributors and growing further through what the career offers them.

This is a true gift — knowing that not only do you make someone feel better personally because of the way she looks and feels using these products, but knowing also that you are giving her confidence, and in many cases a new life, because she has the opportunity to provide for her family and realize her dreams.

We're talking about an opportunity that requires at start-up only a very small application fee, and, based on passion and willingness, offers each woman an unparalleled opportunity to build a business with very little overhead expense. I think that is huge! I would like to be able to do that myself!

I've received gifts from others, and I'm constantly giving — gifts of products and gifts of opportunity. I love gifts! That's what this business is: simply giving away this gift, paying it forward.

I love living and breathing the attitude of giving.

One of the most beautiful stories I've read is contained in "From My Heart to Yours," a book given to me as a gift from Mary Kay Ash. The story is called "The Greatest Gift." It goes something like this:

My friend Paula was given an extravagant Christmas present of a brand new car by her brother. It was beautiful, shiny and sleek (like a SeneCar!). Paula loved the car and drove it to her mother's neighborhood in the older section of the town she grew up in. She parked along the curb in front of her mother's house and went inside to visit with her mother.

After a short while, she noticed a small boy standing on the curb, looking at her sleek new car and admiring it, even touching it and petting if softly, gently, as if it were a prized animal.

Sensing that something significant was happening, Paula stepped out onto the front porch and walked over to the little boy who looked up at her and asked, "Is this your car, lady?"

"Yes," replied Paula, "It was a gift from my brother."

"Your brother gave you a gift of a car like this?" the boy said in genuine amazement. "Hoooo — eeeeee. I sure wish ... "

Paula thought for sure she knew exactly what the little boy would say next, something like he wished he had a brother who would give him something like a car for a present. So the boy's words surprised her ...

"I wish I could be a brother like that to my little sister," he said.

Paula was astonished, and a little ashamed. She asked, "Would you like to have a ride in my new car?" (Of course, Mary Kay shared her version of this story back in the days when you could give a ride to strangers. But it's the message that counts ...)

"You bet I would," the boy exclaimed.

So together in the car they headed off down the street and drove for a couple of blocks. The boy's eyes were lit with joy and he smiled from ear to ear. He turned to Paula and said, "M'am, would you mind pulling up in front of that house over there. That's my home." It was a dilapidated, modest two-story wood frame house that clearly was in great need of repair.

Paula, smiled, knowing, she thought, exactly why the boy wanted to pull in front of his house — to show the neighbors and family that he was riding in such an impressive car on that sunny day.

But she was wrong again.

"Can you stop right here?" the boy exclaimed as Paula pulled the car in front of the house. The boy jumped from the car and ran up the front stoop and into the house.

Paula waited, expecting family and friends to come out and check out the boy's ride. Instead, he came out carrying his little sister, whose legs were in metal braces. The boy sat his sister down at the bottom step and scooted up next to her.

Then he pointed at the car and said, "See Sis? That's the car right there. This kind woman was given that car as a gift from her brother. It was a special present for Christmas, and he gave it to her for nothing! That's the kind of car I'm going to give you someday, with special controls so you can drive it, then together we're going to ride in it downtown and look at all the beautiful things for sale in the shop windows."

When Paula heard this, she was moved to tears. Then she got out of the car, helped the little boy lift his sister into the car and the three of them embarked on a Christmas ride they would never forget.

That was the Christmas when Paula truly came to understand that it is far more blessed to give than to receive.

This beautiful tale reminds me of another called "The Greatest Gift," a short story written by Philip Van Doren Stern more than 60 years ago and adapted by Frank Capra, the legendary film director, into the movie "It's a Wonderful Life."

It's the story of a man who came to understand how important living out our lives is. In fact, the greatest gift of all is this life, in which we are able to lovingly help others.

When Van Doren Stern wrote that story, which became an American classic, he was unable to find a publisher for it. So for Christmas in 1943 he told the story on a Christmas card. He printed 200 copies and gave it as a Christmas gift to friends and family. Eventually the story fell into the hands of Capra, who said he had been looking all his life for such a tale to tell!

Give to others the gifts which you too have been given, and watch your world transform.

❧ Your Turn (Chapter 16) ❧

- What have you done for someone today? If you had to think hard about it, go do something for someone *right now*.

- Have you recently been the recipient of a random act of kindness from someone else? How did it make you feel?

- Purchase extra movie tickets, t-shirts, or seasonal jackets – whatever items you feel you can spend a few extra dollars onevery time you shop. Give them to the families where there are children whose parents cannot afford to spend money on extras. Make a difference in their lives and put a smile on theirfaces. You may be that angel who changes their lives for the best.

Chapter 17
The Business of Beauty

SeneGence products are, to me, about freedom. I don't have to worry about what I look like anymore. As a result of these products, I look perfect all day long. I have great skin. I used to have red, rashy skin and SeneGence products have given me the freedom to have great skin without spending a lot of money. And let me say this about Joni: Joni is an amazing woman; she is sensitive and caring. One time she came to my home for a SeneGence event and the next thing I knew she was serving my mother and father, who live with me. Joni is the same way with our SeneSisters: She doesn't just lead us, she also serves us.

— LETA GREENE, SeneGence Independent Distributor (Royal in Waiting)

This business of beauty is a wonderful business (and it's recession-proof!). It's an inspiring way to make a living because the products we provide are so important in making a woman feel positive about herself.

There have been books written about the business of beauty; some of them detailing the rise to the sales stratosphere of various cosmetics companies. I suggest you read a few to garner an historic perspective on this industry.

The SeneGence SeneBlends Guide to Beauty is a a book available to SeneGence Distributors and does a great job outlining many of the key concepts of skin care and cosmetics of which distributors of beauty products should be aware.

Men generally see women first with their eyes, and the beauty industry is all about doing our best to make that impression a favorable one. First impressions do indeed matter to both men and women alike.

Most women can relate to the business of beauty because they are already customers of somebody's beauty products.

Cosmetics are a very personal product, and direct selling is a very personal sales approach, so there is a natural fit between beauty products and direct sales.

It's easy to understand why some women who become SeneGence Independent Distributors love hosting Glamour Demos, the ultimate personal selling venue. To them, that is the business. The Glamour Demo is the primary place where selling happens, because guests are seeing the products up close and being offered the chance to purchase products of choice. It's fun to get together with other women and do something so "girly." It's so much fun that distributors can forget that there is business that is happening at these product "parties."

The enthusiastic Distributor who has wowed and scheduled a Glamour Demo already knows there is work in filling the event with plenty of new friends and guests, and ensuring appointments actually are conducted on the original date scheduled. Somehow, the Distributor wowed someone with the product on the back of her hand, exchanged phone numbers and followed through to "book" them and coach her hostess on how to hold a successful event. At the demo, the real work begins. It's fun, but it's work.

This is where the results of the "business of beauty" really begin to manifest for the SeneGence Independent Distributor.

Let's talk about what happens at a SeneGence demo. If you're a seasoned SeneGence Independent Distributor, you already know most of this (I hope!). If not, well, here comes some inside info.

It starts by recognizing there are at least three different types of demos: the Glamour Demo, the SeneBlend Demo and the Launch Demo (Note: Throughout this book I capitalize "Glamour Demo" to help you follow along when we're talking about a SeneGence event).

The Glamour Demo is the "workhorse" of SeneGence demos. It is where the SeneGence product and opportunity typically comes to the public arena in most selling situations. The Glamour

Demo consists of a SeneGence Independent Distributor, a Hostess, and three or more other adult guests. There are four specific goals of this type of demo:

1. **Help the Hostess earn products and her SeneGift (as a "thank you" for hosting).**
2. **Identify new customers and sell products.**
3. **Identify and sign up new Distributors**
4. **Book future demos.**

At the Glamour Demo, guests learn about SeneGence product technologies and sample textures on the backs of their hands. The SeneGence Independent Distributor leading the Glamour Demo teaches them about the products and their functions, unique characteristics and uses as outlined in the *SeneGence Beauty Book*, a standard reference of the product lineup. Every guest will apply LipSense lip color (won't rub, smear or kiss off) to her lips prior to the end of the Glamour Demo.

Toward the end of the Glamour Demo, guests are given the opportunity to purchase any products they desire, and also book a follow-up SeneBlend Demo (one-on-one; see below) or another Glamour Demo, or sometimes both based on the choice they've made to either become a customer of the product or a distributor of the product (see page 130 for Glamour Demo Illustration).

The next demo category is the **SeneBlend Demo**. Most of the time this is not an introductory demo, but is a follow-up to the Glamour Demo.

A SeneBlend Demo consists of a SeneGence Independent Distributor and one or two other women. If the guest at a Glamour Demo chooses to become a customer of SeneGence products, the presenting SeneGence Independent Distributor will book the future SeneBlend Demo to teach the new customer proper color application, placement and various glamour techniques learned at various SeneGence events throughout the year.

This is an opportunity for the Distributor to spend more one-on-one time with the customer, establishing a more intimate relationship, and an opportunity to present the full product line (perhaps more sales). Remember, color application and placement begins with clean, moisturized skin. So the Distributor always takes the opportunity to present SeneGence cleansing and moisturizing products, if she hasn't already done so.

The SeneBlend Demo is usually held privately at a date and time when the customer and the Distributor can spend at least an hour without interruption.

The third category of demo for the SeneGence Independent Distributor is **the Launch Demo.** This is a Glamour Demo conducted by the upline sponsor for a new SeneGence Independent Distributor who likely signed up at a previous Glamour Demo or SeneBlend Demo. This is the upline sponsor's chance to show her new Distributor how a demo is conducted, to pass on the tricks of the trade that the SeneGence Independent Distributor has learned through experience, through her own upline, and through learning by doing.

By the way, the *SeneGence Beauty Book* is a product-by-product guide that teaches the features and benefits of the SeneGence product line, and it was specially designed to assist a Distributor in conducting a Glamour Demo. In fact, there is even a Distributor Guide (our "cheat sheet") to accompany the SeneGence Beauty Book, advising a new Distributor on exactly what to say at her Glamour Demos.

Studies have shown that in our current marketplace it is important to let consumers know about a company and its products before offering them the opportunity to make a purchase. The *SeneGence Beauty Book* helps the Distributor review this information at the beginning of the

Glamour Demo. For example,

• The who, what and why of SeneGence are discussed in a section titled "Vision."

• The who, what and why of the products are revealed in the "Products" section. This is the section the Distributor uses as a guide for the actual demo.

• Consumers rightfully demand that corporations take responsibility for the impact their businesses have on the environment and the community. SeneGence reveals its positions in the "Environment and Community" section of the book.

• Today's consumers generally require and find delight in the benefit of the extra perks offered with the use of a company's service or product. SeneGence has designed the Hostess Appreciation Program and SeneGift for just such reasons, and it's detailed in the book.

• The days of unsubstantiated product claims are over. The well-informed consumers of today want to know how the products work and they need to know what benefits they can expect to receive. The hows and whats of SeneGence are covered in the "Skincare and Independent Clinical Test Results" section of the book.

I think you can see just how important the *SeneGence Beauty Book* is. I tell SeneGence Independent Distributors to use it at every Glamour Demo.

Above all, as I've mentioned elsewhere in this book, the most important point in every Glamour Demo is to offer each participant the SeneGence Choice – to become either a customer of the products or a Distributor.

A big component of every demo – especially the Glamour Demo – is to take time to learn about each one of the guests in order to help each understand which choice might be best for her. I like to say that SeneGence is a "high touch" company with "high technologies." High touch means building relationships with customers and downline Distributors. If you are a SeneGence Independent Distributor, you should feel privileged to have an opportunity to get to know each of your guests: their lifestyles, work situations, family/children issues, etc.

If guests believe that you are genuinely interested in them as individuals, they will be more willing to receive the information and advice you offer. You are usually the only one at the demo who already understands the opportunities that lie ahead for the guests.

Taking an interest in the guests at a Glamour Demo makes every demo fun and different. Discover which guests work with women, are involved in women's organizations or do volunteer work. Who loves to stay busy? Who is very social? Who is searching for something more?

Then, as you learn about each guest, you constantly reinforce the individual and unique opportunities SeneGence provides each the guest specifically. For example, maybe a guest tells you she is a high school teacher. You might respond, "Oh my goodness! You need to choose to become a Distributor! You have a built-in customer base at work. How many of the other teachers at your school are women? Don't you think they would just love this product that lasts the entire school day?"

The *SeneGence Independent Distributor Demo Guide* is an online book available to every SeneGence Independent Distributor. It is free, and filled with time-proven techniques for conducting successful Glamour Demos, with everything from preparing for the demo to how to set up product displays and how to follow up after a Glamour Demo.

The point I hope I've made here is that the Glamour Demo is the cornerstone of the direct-sales beauty business, because it is here that fun and several forms of future income mix. The Business of Beauty can become for you as bountiful as you choose.

Of course, there is a lot more to building a successful business, such as customer service and administrative operations. I'll cover some of those in the next chapters.

❧ Your Turn (Chapter 17) ❧

• Can you now name the three basic types of demos used in the SeneGence system of selling and sponsoring? If not, go back and reread the previous chapter. Now list each of three basic SeneGence demos and the goals of each.

• Recall a product demonstration you've been to recently that was fun and engaging. Maybe it was a product party for a direct-selling opportunity, maybe even your most recent SeneGence demo. Maybe it was a food demonstration at a supermarket or a cool new product on display at the mall. What made the experience fun? Keep a list of fun ideas you can duplicate in your business.

• SeneGence Independent Distributors: Have you visited the "back office" section of www.senegence.com? Have you looked at or downloaded the *SeneGence Independent Distributor Demo Guide*? Go back and reread it today, and then make a short list of 2-3 ideas you will incorporate in your next Demo (which is, hopefully, this week!).

Chapter 18
Customers are Worth Their Weight in Gold

Simply by helping another woman get more organized and focused upon a certain outcome you are contributing in a positive way to the quality of her life.

— JONI

As I've said elsewhere, the direct-sales multilevel marketer has two distinct types of customers. We're not just selling products, we're also offering each customer the opportunity to become a seller (Distributor) of these products herself.

The time that you spend with either type of customer is always precious. Maybe the first time you meet a new customer or prospect at a demo you spend one hour with her. Your relationship may begin with that one-hour meeting, but that customer might become a customer for the next 10 years. Or longer!

So the one hour you spent with a prospective new customer might very well actually be worth its weight in gold.

She might first appear as a customer with the purchase of a set of lip products, and as she grows confident in the product performance and in her relationship with you she might typically progress to the skin-care products, the bath products, and so on. Her original lip-set order of $45, for example, might eventually turn into ordering $1,000 and even more over the next 10 years! So become committed to making that very first meeting a successful experience for her. You want to have as many customers as possible who grow and spend thousands of dollars over each 10-year period.

That's what I mean when I say the customer is worth her weight in gold!

Customers are our business. That may be true in every business, but in direct selling women's cosmetics it's even more important to understand this. And in multilevel marketing you always keep in mind that the customer who chooses to become a Distributor will contribute the most to your long-term financial freedom and success, because she and the women she sponsors will continue to generate and grow commission income for you. Seek out those customers who will become Distributors and let the others default to being long-term loyal customers.

I was very focused on this fact when I started in direct sales more than 20 years ago. I stepped into understanding this truth: Real long-term success is earned by building downline Distributors who in turn sponsor new Distributors who then bring in multiples of new retail customers. That's called "exponential growth." That is multiplying your efforts.

I could see that the first thing I had to perfect in this business was the art of doing a demo, so I could then teach my downline Distributors how to do what I do, and then the multiplication tables would take over. My goal is to teach other women that the promise of freedom, independence and financial success in direct sales is realized through the fundamental day-to-day activities of conducting Glamour Demos and building a downline organization of Distributors.

Every woman who sells SeneGence or other direct-sales products should understand this important strategy for building wealth. Otherwise, they will lack a long-term vision of how big this career can actually become when the right company offers long-term sustainability and earning potential.

It is said that women get caught up in the moment, focusing on making immediate income as opposed to building for the future. But I believe in making long-term investments on a daily basis, for long-term exponential gain, which is a far greater return. The short-term sale puts cash in hand, at the Glamour Demo, and it's about a 20 percent to 55 percent profit for the retail sale in hand because of the product discount you have earned by being a SeneGence Distributor. So for many women that cash is immediate, obvious and very practical. It doesn't take many cash sales at a couple of Glamour Demos each month before you have enough cash in hand to pay the mortgage or rent check for the month. That's what I call an immediate payoff. Building a downline of customers who are also Distributors, on the other hand, takes a while to start paying off but when it does, the earnings really begin to increase as new Distributors you may have never met become members of your downline – through exponential growth.

I recently listened to an astute sales guru talking about what is called a "future build." The success stories of individuals who make millions in direct sales focus knowingly, or in some cases "accidentally," on the idea of a "future build."

This particular concept reminds me of the story of Mark Zuckerberg, who founded Facebook in early 2004. Facebook began as a small network that students at Harvard University could use to communicate with one another.

At the time, Zuckerberg was lucky to even be at Harvard because just months before his website of student photos landed him in hot water with the Harvard University administration.

The following summer, Zuckerberg and a few friends moved to California and continued tinkering with their Facebook idea. While there, they met an investor who was willing to fund them and their idea to the tune of half a million dollars.

Do you know when Facebook finally became cash-flow positive? It was in the fall of 2009 – more than five years after the business was started! Apparently, year after year they struggled to pay for basic expenses but believed their endeavor would eventually pay off in a big way.

At one point in 2006, giant Yahoo even attempted to acquire Facebook for $1 billion! That's a lot of gold for a company that wasn't even making money. Zuckerberg said "no" and instantly became famous as "the kid who turned down a billion dollars."

But Zuckerberg and his partners and investors had their eyes and hearts fixed firmly on this idea of "future build," because that is exactly what they were doing: building the future by building an infrastructure with data servers and building a following of loyal and young clients.

Imagine ... by 2007 Facebook was valued at more than $15 billion, but had annual revenue of only $150 million. In 2010, Facebook reached about half a billion users.

By the way, Zuckerberg, who accomplished all this well before reaching age 30, did not complete college at Harvard. Nevertheless, his story of success serves as a great inspiration for all of us.

A woman who chooses to become a SeneGence Distributor can easily imagine a successful future because there is no need to experience a loss. Ever.

Start the "business of beauty" by hosting a Glamour Demo at which products are sold, costs are covered and profits are earned. Continue building your future income by continually wowing, booking and demo-ing, and by focusing on building a downline of women who also want this direct-sales opportunity. At the same time, you will encounter plenty of women who choose to become customers, who only want to purchase your products.

Either way, you are going to have to accept their money (wink, wink), whether they just want the product or they want to become Distributors themselves. In this manner of business building, positive cash flow from the very beginning is a sure outcome.

Be thankful for customers who want the product but not the opportunity. After all, we have a great product, and it is this type of customer who makes it possible for our business to grow by providing to us immediate cash flow to pay for our near-term necessities as we build long-term growth for the future.

In my experience only about 5 percent of the women who enter into the business of direct selling understand this opportunity of "future build" by building an organization of downline Distributors. I have a great deal of respect for women who join our company only to earn money from immediate sales, and who build their careers only selling and not sponsoring and building, because even these women have demonstrated the courage to break away from the traditional employment/paycheck model, become their own bosses and chart their own courses.

With all of this emphasis on the importance of both retail and opportunity customers, it's worth mentioning some of the most important ways that Distributors provide service to each.

For the retail customer, basic good customer service is simply giving that person your attention when she needs it. This could mean giving her instruction and guidance on color application, or helping her with product placement such as how to draw an eyebrow. Or, she may need support from you to understand that moisturizing her face using your products will make her look younger and more refreshed.

Your customer may call you to help her prepare for a big date or for makeup application help for a family wedding. You'll want to be ready with tips on the right mascara, on choosing the right shadow or highlighter for a sunny day, or how to blend colors to look her best in those wedding day photographs that will spend a lifetime hanging on her sister's living room wall. Here is your opportunity to truly be of service to your customer.

This kind of customer service can change your life. You will make lifelong friends by helping these customers use your beauty products during these life-changing events.

Attentive and caring service for your customer who has chosen to become a Distributor herself has similar satisfactions. You are helping this person remember to go to trainings, get organized, schedule and set priorities that help her become a better mom, a better wife and a better businesswoman. Simply by helping another women become more organized and more focused upon a certain outcome allows you to contribute in a positive way to the quality of her life.

We offer a very personal level of service to the SeneGence SenseCosmetics and SeneDerm Skincare customer who is fretting over her wedding. Give as much attention as possible to women who want help — they are retail customers and downline Distributors. You frequently find these women at SeneGence Glamour Demos and trainings.

Spend 50 percent of your time helping women one-on-one in a manner that serves their needs. That service pays off exponentially by helping them become either exceptional customers of the product or exceptional Distributors who in turn apply these same techniques to their own downline organizations, upon which your commission income continues to grow.

This kind of allegiance, and the relationship value between a company and its Distributors, as well as between the Distributors and their customers, really became evident during a critical time in the history of SeneGence.

We call it the "Popper Stopper Incident."

The "poppers" were the tops of LipSense lip color tubes that started popping off their tops as a result of a manufacturing error in 2003. We were not aware of the situation until hundreds of calls and e-mails started flooding in, complaining of ruined purses, stained carpets and clothes ... oh my goodness! We investigated immediately and found millions of dollars worth of inventory that was produced with the malfunctioning "poppers."

The problem, the extent of the damage and its cause became apparent to us the day after our annual Seminar meeting. I realized the only thing we could do was to call our Distributor leaders back to California to help out. We set up a call-center right in our headquarters office lobby and set up tables, chairs and telephones. Then the leaders, along with company employees and me, started calling every single Distributor for SeneGence, explaining the problem and asking the number of LipSense tubes still in their possession so that we could send them "proper poppers" that would correct the defect. The leaders returned happily to California (at their own expense!) and sat in our lobby making calls for three full days.

What could have destroyed our new startup company made us stronger as a result of strong relationships and great customer service. Proof positive: Our customers are worth more than their weight in gold.

⤳ Your Turn (Chapter 18) ⤳

• Use your favorite Web search engine and type in the following searches:

    a) "long-term customer value"

    b) "how much is a customer really worth"

    c) "how to lose customers"

• Do you know what a conversion rate is in sales? If not, try searching the Web for an answer.

• Go to your local library or bookstore and check out a copy of BusinessWeek Magazine or Entrepreneur Magazine. Or pick up a copy of a publication such as Direct Selling News. Find a success story. Now read the article carefully and figure out how customers played the main role in the company's success.

Chapter 19
The Art of Selling

The art of selling is about elevating the work that you do to a higher plane. You're elevating your work into art by turning your motivations away from a quick buck and instead focusing on acts of kindness for others. This is the true art of selling!

— JONI

If wowing, booking, demo-ing and directing customers and Distributors represent the *science* of successful direct selling, then there is also an *art* of direct selling. The most successful direct sellers work on both the science *and* the art of selling.

In other words, you've got to employ both sides of your brain to make it all work together. Use the techniques outlined in this book as a structure for your selling approach. Then work on your creative side to fully realize the art to this business too!

The art of selling is about transforming the sales presentation into a magical, engaging and, most of all, meaningful, validating experience for every customer, Distributor and potential Distributor. This is where you become more than just a seller; you become a friend, a consultant, a confidant and a mentor. Accomplish this by applying creativity and imagination to the sales process, and by learning to be of service to others.

Has your local real estate agent ever placed small flags near your driveway on the Fourth of July? How about a local florist promoting graduation bouquets and graduation rehearsal arrangements? Ever noticed how your local hardware store starts promoting barbeque grills around late spring?

These are all examples of sales campaigns based on seasonal

themes. And direct sellers will attest that seasonal campaigns work. Sellers know that when seasons change and customers' emotions and generosity are ramped up, this is a very good time to sell something. Holidays, graduations, weddings and so on – all are prime opportunities to increase otherwise normal sales.

Mitsuwa Market, a large Japanese market in Southern California, promotes a broiled eel sale just prior to the Midsummer Day of the Ox. Beverage companies focus national campaigns on holidays and seasons. And the creative cosmetics seller wants to do likewise during the holidays, turning these days into opportunities.

There are so many special days, weeks and months of the year set aside for so many different types of events, celebrations, people and lifestyles! Enough so you could literally never run out of enough great ideas to engage in special promotions. Check them out yourself by using a computer search engine such as Google, searching under "list of special days" for starters.

The list of opportunities for those who, like our SeneGence Independent Distributors, sell cosmetics and other beauty products, goes well beyond the standards such as Valentine's Day or Mother's Day (which, of course, still are and always will be lovely occasions for a customer to pick up a lip, personal care or skincare product or collection for mom or a sister.) And for husbands and dads, male skin care products and fragrances are ideal!

Did you know there's a "Clean Hands Week?" It's in September. And it's perfect for promoting hand moisturizing lotions and cleansers. "Smile Week"? It's in August, and presents a great sales opportunity for lip products and lip colors. There is even a "Wear Red Day," in February. Though it's not Valentine's Day, it's a perfect time to purchase a perfect shade of the hottest LipSense color.

SeneGence Independent Distributors can go to the company's "back-office" website to find a list of special seasonal promotions, including marketing materials they can download and customize to create local sales promotions for their own customers and distributors.

Other direct-selling companies create similar promotions for their distributors (If your company doesn't, it's time to ask why!).

Promotions often include printed material such as flyers, signs or banners to help reinforce a special sales message to customers. Amid the noise and general busyness of most people's lives, it's important to use these tools to break through the clutter. SeneGence offers its Distributors access to flyers and other special promotion tools that can be downloaded from the company website.

Special flyers and printed promotional support tools can often help the customer communicate her need to her Distributor. For example, a customer recently called one of our SeneGence Independent Distributors to place a reorder for the "gooey stuff" she purchased previously. Through sharing information on a flyer the Distributor previously left with the customer, it was determined the "gooey stuff" was actually our Glossy Lip Moisturizer!

The art of selling is more than selling certain products at certain times of the year. The art of selling is also about elevating the work you do to a higher plane. You're elevating your work into art by turning your motivations away from a quick buck and instead focusing on acts of kindness for others. This is the true art of selling!

Learn to listen and to cultivate a genuine interest in others. There's a cute little slide show you can view on the Web at www.theartofsellingmovie.com that promotes the idea that successful selling is not about selling at all; it's about giving to others and being of service to people and building a network of trust. I happen to believe that is right on the money. And it's a fact that, all other things being equal, most people will do business with the person or company they trust over the competition.

I like how my role model and mentor Tony Robbins puts

it: "Life is a gift, and it offers us the privilege, opportunity and responsibility to give something back by becoming more."

I am among those who have heard those words and live it as a way of life.

Blend science (the facts) and art (personality, character, presentation and design intentions) in your selling style and make "becoming more" possible.

❧ Your Turn (Chapter 19) ❧

• Imagine you own a dry-cleaning business (or even a cosmetics business) with a single store. Can you think of five special promotions yo could run during the year associated with major holidays or special occasions? How would you promote and advertise them without spending a lot of money?

• If you haven't already done so, visit *www.theartofsellingmovie.com* right now.

• Are you trustworthy? Do you give to others freely?

• Think about what Tony Robbins says: "Life is a gift, and it offers us the privilege, opportunity and responsibility to give something back by becoming more." Can you list three ways you have given to others recently and, in each case, what you got back in return?

Chapter 20
The Prudent Shopkeeper

Having the opportunity to work at SeneGence, and more importantly, with Joni, has allowed me to grow both professionally and personally. Joni started SeneGence with a vision of finding a unique product to help women become independent and successful in their own business. Thankfully, she included me in the process. Joni is a woman I deeply admire and respect, and has been my mentor and friend over these past years. I will be forever in her debt.

— LINDA BAILEY, First SeneGence Employee

There is no skill in direct sales more important than that of being a prudent shopkeeper – that is, managing inventory to build and support your business.

It's not nearly as sexy a subject as, say, how to demo beauty products or how to wow and dazzle prospects.

But make no mistake; inventory management will separate the girls from the women in direct sales every time. Master this skill, and you are poised for powerful payoffs.

It's all about having the correct amount of product, of inventory, on hand at all times, or at the very least, making that your goal.

When a customer asks for a product you don't have on hand, you either lose a sale (it's called "impulse buying" for a reason) or it will cost you more – at least 50 to 75 percent more – to fulfill an order. That 50 to 75 percent comes out of your potential profits. Somebody has to pay for shipping and handling, not to mention delivery.

To avoid this and to maximize your profits, begin your career with enough inventory to service each woman you will see within a two-week period. If you cannot do this, begin an inventory build-up by using your customers' money as the investment money to do so. I did this to build SeneGence. Remember the trade shows I talked about working in Chapter 3?

When you're just starting out, there may be times when you simply can't manage your supply ordering well enough to be prepared always for the immediate sale. SeneGence provides a "Demo Drop Ship" program for this reason. But bear in mind every time you ship a product directly to a customer instead of delivering it yourself, you lose another opportunity to "upsell" and to reinforce your value.

On the other hand, when you deliver an order in person to a customer at work, for example, you have an opportunity to meet other women in your customer's workplace, and perhaps identify new customers or prospects for Demos. Or maybe you notice your customer isn't very busy; that things at work aren't going very well. This is a perfect opportunity to suggest she may want to try her hand at selling these fantastic products you are delivering to her.

This is one of the most important lessons in direct sales that you can learn, and it's a major reason why direct sales will always have an advantage over retail selling in stores.

The prudent shopkeeper lives by two important principles:

1. Deliver products personally, and at the product demo whenever possible.

2. Build inventory by reinvesting early profits into additional inventory, remembering that you are investing in your own future. Do this for at least for the first six months or a year of your business, depending upon the number of demos you expect to

conduct over a two week period. (Take into consideration reorder products and campaigns, too.)

There is no magic formula. But if you're doing two or more demos a week, and supporting customer reorders, you're going to order, over time or all at once if you can, somewhere between $5,000 and $20,000 in inventory to maximize your business opportunity. Some use their own money, others use their customers' money.

Here's the math: You have weekly sales of $1,000. That means each week you are selling somewhere around $500 of inventory, with your cost of goods sold at a 50 percent discount from suggested retail. That leaves $500 profit. So what should you do with that $500 profit?

I urge you to be a prudent shopkeeper.

The prudent shopkeeper will exercise restraint, paying out to herself only a set stipend for each demo she conducts. The rest? The prudent shopkeeper invests most of the profits from her demo back into inventory until the desired inventory level has been achieved. That's an "inventory build." She might keep, say, $50 per demo. The prudent shopkeeper measures her payoff in a set amount per activity, not a percentage of that activity.

Remember, if you're selling products (which is a very good thing!), you're moving inventory out of your "store" inventory. We're assuming you have to have a large enough inventory to cover your two, maybe three demos a week for a two-week period. Even so, you're going to have to be repurchasing inventory to keep pace with what you are selling and replace items. So you're constantly replenishing, if not building, inventory.

That is, if you're a prudent shopkeeper.

Consider this: In the first year of sales at SeneGence we took in $1.7 million. Me? I took $100 a week to buy groceries. The rest went to building inventory and funding the business. The lesson I've learned is, "Start where you are and build from there. But for heaven's sake get started!" It doesn't matter where you start or how much money you have. You start from there and build by being a prudent shopkeeper.

Your "store" has to be stocked if you want to make money. There is no secret to getting rich quickly. That's not how this works. You build. And build. And build. Imagine what they had to build at Facebook before their business was ready to "take off."

During your first year or two of direct sales, you can make a living, but generally speaking, not a fortune. Be patient. Reinvest. Become a prudent shopkeeper for as long as it takes, and remember no two direct-sales businesses are the same.

So how much inventory do you need in your "store?" The correct answer is based on how many new customers you plan to service at Glamour Demos and their reorder volume, taking into consideration additional events or sales campaigns you plan over the course of a two-week period.

As it applies to reorders, calculate what the value and content of reorders will likely be from those customers, and figure in expanded product-usage growth as you introduce body-care products, hair-care products and maybe aromatherapeutics to existing clients.

And, of course, you're planning to expand your customers' product selection and usage as a result of your promotional campaigns. I suggest at least one sales campaign per month, or simply extend the company's product campaign to your clients to keep it simple.

So it's difficult to say exactly how much inventory you will need now or in the future. But you will work at it and figure out the perfect amount of inventory required that is best for you.

You'll want to sit down and figure out how many new customers you need each week to attain your financial goals. If you want to make, say, $300 a week, you have to determine how you are going to do that. Are you going to generate income at Glamour Demos? If so, you have to estimate how many women must attend those demos, based on nine out of 10 women buying products at the Demo. This is where coaching the hostess comes into play. Every distributor must set her own goals, do her own math and determine exactly what her precise inventory needs will be.

Remember, you will sell more when you have inventory available at the Glamour Demo at the moment your customer wants to buy. And your costs for delivery of the product will never be lower than at the Glamour Demo. On-the-spot delivery maximizes earnings.

So there you have it. Inventory plays a major role in the success of earning sales income and generating excited and loyal customers.

My first, and biggest, lesson in prudent shopkeeping came 25 years ago when I first started out in direct sales.

I was very excited about my new career as an independent skin-care consultant, of course.

I had no savings while I was working full time and attending college classes, living with my parents in Yorba Linda, California. My dad was at that time vice president of merchandising for Sav-On Drugs. I was going to place my very first cosmetics inventory order so that I could begin the sales process.

I still remember that evening when my dad walked in from work. He could tell I was excited about something I was doing with all of these papers, including the product-order forms, spread out before me on the kitchen table.

Dad asked, "Joni Rae, what are you doing?"

When I told him, he asked to have a look at my work and quickly scanned the numbers I had scrawled on the form.

"You're only ordering one of everything," he said.

"I know," I replied. "I'm going to build a display so people can see what I'm talking about when I teach them about the products."

He frowned and said, "Joni Rae, have I taught you nothing? You cannot sell from an empty wagon!" Then he smiled slightly and added, "Let me see that order form."

He took the form and started making notes. He read that the company was a Direct Selling Association (DSA) member (SeneGence is too), and he read about the standard DSA guarantee to buy back 90 percent of unsold inventory.

He said, "Look, Joni Rae, you have nothing to lose – this product is guaranteed. I will lend you $5,000 and you will pay me back on a weekly basis. At least it will give you something to start with so that you have some inventory in your store."

So I placed the order that evening with dad's help, and I soon received 12 boxes of cosmetics and supplies.

I hardly knew what was in those boxes. I had never even seen a demonstration of the product. Twelve boxes! From the very start of the first demonstration I carried those boxes along with me to every demo I conducted. I carried those boxes up the steps to my first demo, and I stacked them up against the wall and went to town, nervous, stumbling and simply reading a "flip chart" that explained products and usage instructions. Every woman in that room kept looking at those boxes, and each one had no doubt she was going to be taking home some products at the end of the evening, because there it was, looming over there, filling the wall space!

Talk about success! Not only did I tell them I had inventory, but they were looking at it throughout the evening! It was like a feeding frenzy in a shark tank. The guests at my classes would witness the selling of so much product, they would do the quick math, and then they would approach me and ask me how much money I made and ask, "Can you teach me how to do that?"

I would respond, "Sure, fill out this agreement and write a

check for $5,000 and I'll show you how to do a demo the way I do it." And that's all I knew how to do. And sure enough, they soon became successful too following this approach ... creating a duplicable cycle of success with lots of people jumping on board to earn money part time.

I repaid my dad, giving him a couple hundred dollars each week, after which I owned the inventory on the shelf outright. His loan to me served as a "credit card purchase" that I paid off with customers' money over time.

So, if you have the capital to begin your business with a full inventory, that's the best way to start in this business.

However, let me be completely clear: You don't necessarily have to start out with a large investment, or much of any investment at all. Remember, you start wherever you are. It's great to build your business on someone else's capital, but sometimes it just isn't possible, and you start your initial inventory using your credit card and whatever you have available.

Do your best to build an inventory level until you can readily sell all products at every Glamour Demo.

If necessary, use a credit card and set yourself on a scheduled repayment plan. Tell yourself, "I'm going to make, say, $200 in profits each week for myself." Then make payments on the credit card until the balance is down to zero. Along the way, use the money you have left to order additional products to build your inventory level.

Suppose you don't have a credit card, savings or a friend or relative who believes in you and who will give you a short-term loan like my dad did for me. With SeneGence you can still get started using our Customer Direct Order (CDO) process. You conduct the Glamour Demo, take the orders and place each guest's order by clicking on the "Purchase Products Now" button on the home page at SeneGence. com using the customer's credit card. SeneGence will ship the product directly to your customer and issue you a check for your portion of the sales income commission.

Of course, with CDO you lose the advantage of on-the-spot sales, but again, you have to start where you are. If you're using CDO, you are reinvesting your sales income amounts mostly into building an inventory so you can eventually sell from a full wagon and therefore sell even more. Just like dad said!

So regardless of where the start-up capital comes from, who pays for your business? Your customers do! While you build your business. Think Donald Trump. The Rockefellers. Mark Zuckerberg of Facebook. They built their businesses using other peoples' money. These business icons are examples of "prudent shopkeepers," and so too will you be!

❧ Your Turn (Chapter 20) ❧

• Ok, here is your math quiz ... You have a product you sell for $100. You sell an average of three of these products a week. It costs $25 to ship a single product to a customer and $15 to ship each additional product to a customer, as long as they are shipped at the same time. You have a maxed out credit card that you can pay down by $250 next month. And a convention you're attending next month at which you expect you can obtain 15 orders for your product. Of those 15, seven customers will likely ask to have their product shipped and the other eight will want delivery at the show. Now, here's the math: How many products should you carry with you to the convention? The answer: Well, it's a lot more complicated than we have time for here, but I would bring at least 10, and be ready to use most the profit from those 10 sales to pay down your credit card immediately. Then use the credit card to place or finalize the remaining seven orders for follow-up shipment. Wow! See what being a prudent shopkeeper involves?

• Are you at your credit's end? Well, can you list three people (friends, family members, etc.) who will give you a short-term loan knowing that you are purchasing for direct-sales inventory? Remember, according to DSA guidelines your product purchase is refundable up to 90 percent of your last product purchase if you do not succeed in selling. Be prepared with a copy of your business plan and/or your company's compensation plan. I bet you can name three people who would be willing to help you get started.

Chapter 21
Getting Organized at Home

Joni and SeneGence have provided me with an incredible avenue for personal financial independence while being part of a large family: the SeneGence community of Distributors. I have grown tremendously as a representative for this amazing product line, all while making special friends along the way. I can't imagine my life without Joni, SeneGence and the faithful friendships I have developed. It has been an amazing journey that I pray will continue for years to come.

— BRIDGETTE LAMBROS, SeneGence Independent Distributor (Countess)

If you are going to remain sane and also have a successful direct-selling career, you must master the skill of carefully planning both your personal and business time.

This doesn't mean you become a compulsive clock-watcher or a minute-miser who only and always does things on schedule like an android in a 1970s movie. No, the reason you are seeking a career in direct sales is because you desire freedom, independence and the ability to live creatively and flexibly, balancing work with home, family, health and the other interests in your life.

Ironically, although you are seeking an escape from a routine life or career, you will be traveling across galaxies toward the final goal of freedom and success by adding a few routines to managing your time and priorities.

For SeneGence Independent Distributors, the SeneGence *Book to Build with Basic Selling Principles* outlines the steps you need to take to get your life and your direct-selling career in tip-top order. It's a matter of setting priorities, and SeneGence Independent Distributors can continually check and recheck their prioritization planning by referring to "Book to Build" training over and over again at the SeneGence Website in the Distributor "back office." Contained in that collection of writings is pretty much everything you need to know about how to plan your time and priorities in both your personal life and in your business career.

In this chapter and the next, I'd like to cover the basics of the Book to Build life- and business-management process. If you become a SeneGence Independent Distributor, or already are one, I assume you will want to dig into these truths much more deeply in the SeneGence *Book to Build*. There's a lot of reading here so feel free to take your time and maybe read this chapter in sections. Use a highlighter if you want, and make note of the areas to come back to and reread as you gradually bring order to chaos in your life.

I still remember the old days when cars like my favorite 1968 Ford Mustang used to have a single-wheel drive system. Those were the days when hot-rodders in high school could get one of the car's rear wheels spinning by just hitting the gas from a standing start. Since all of the engine's power was transferred to a single wheel, they would get that one rear tire spinning and smoking in the school parking lot, usually with a crowd of other kids looking on and shouting "Whoa! Cool." If you're a Baby Boomer, you probably remember what I'm talking about.

But along came the 1990s, and the next thing you knew almost all the cars around had front-wheel drive, and even the ones with rear-wheel drive had fancy new systems that transferred power to both rear wheels, making it almost impossible to get those tires spinning without going anywhere. Now two wheels were pushing or pulling your car instead of just one. And having those two wheels working together made cars a lot safer, sure-footed and easier to drive safely. That's what having two wheels, rather than one, can do for you.

The same applies to managing your business and personal time. You need two "wheels": one to manage your personal time and priorities, and one to do likewise with your business priorities. Each of the two wheels reflects your priorities in life, though in different arenas. And you must have both to have balance.

Allow me to introduce you to two wheels: The Life Balance Wheel and The Business Balance Wheel. Get to know both of them, and you will be on your way to becoming happy, successful and more worry-free. Each of your two new wheels – The Life Balance Wheel and The Business Balance Wheel – can be viewed as wheels representing areas of your life, divided into sections, with spokes radiating from a hub. The spokes represent aspects of your life or career.

1. Getting Your Life in Balance

Look first at the Life Balance Wheel (page 210, Fig. 1). Begin by asking yourself, "What is important to me?" Remember, we asked this of ourselves way back in Chapter 8 – "What Do You Really Want?" Now it's time to dig a little deeper.

Do you ever wonder where does the time go? Do you ever start a day, live the day, and by the end of the day realize nothing was accomplished? Do you feel as though you spent the day simply "maintaining" as opposed to forging ahead closer to completing projects that bring you that much closer to your goal?

Developing good time management habits based on The Life Balance Wheel will greatly reduce wasted time, make your days more productive and help you to achieve your goals. If you take the time to initiate good time-management practices, you will find you not only achieve more each day but you will also have more energy, feel more confident and enjoy a fuller life. As good time-management practices become a way of life, you will also find more time to enjoy activities and interests in which you previously did not have time to indulge.

Adopting a commitment to execute good time-management

Sample Life Balance Wheel

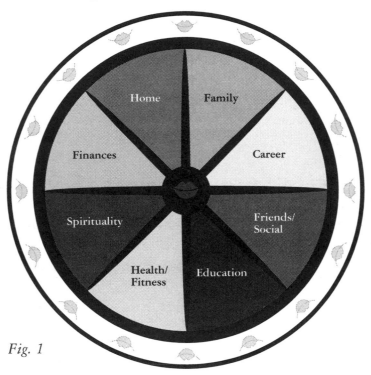

Fig. 1

practices will enhance your quality of life. Good time-management habits improve your private life, your professional life, your leisure life and virtually every other part of your existence, giving you an astonishing sense of accomplishment.

You simply must get organized. It may take a small investment of your time, and even your money, right now, to purchase items that will help to make your life more efficient and organized. This small investment will pay you back with big dividends. The decisions you make by analyzing and implementing organizational skills will sharpen your focus, eliminate much clutter (mental and tangible) and set up the foundation of good time-management practices. The time you gain will free your mind and body to pursue your goals.

Clutter of the mind makes you feel tired and slows you down. Successful individuals know it is impossible to keep a well organized, continually updated list of projects and things to do in your mind. There are too many projects to work on and too many tasks associated with those projects. Write down projects and related tasks required to complete the project successfully on a piece of paper, or enter it into a list on your PDA, laptop, iPad, or PC. This alone will free your mind to work toward solutions and take on tasks to complete the projects.

As you eliminate clutter in your life, you will also engage in setting priorities for what remains. Don't just set priorities, set them by category. Some of the areas of your life that might require attention, streamlining and prioritization include:

- **Home:** Laundry, Cleaning, Clothing, Groceries, Gardening, Bills

- **Family/Personal:** Errands, Entertainment, Education, Lifestyle, Meals

- **Work:** Paper Work, Bills, Correspondence, Primary Job Function

- **Social:** Correspondence, Phone Calls, Social Appointments

The quest to organize each of these areas can be daunting. It might be more palatable to tackle these segments one at a time; perhaps one per weekend might work for you. If the project is huge, like organizing a kitchen or an entire billing-record filing cabinet, you may want to divide it into groupings to be done at intervals.

The critical issue is to begin to save time. As you conquer each of these categories, make a list of items you require to complete the project. Keep the list with you at all times. Delegate a small portion of your new income to purchase the items you have identified, one-by-one. It may take a year to complete this process. Again, the point is to begin today, amidst where you are in your life this very moment.

To make this entire process easier you need to meet two more new best (and imaginary) friends: **Bocks** (pronounced "Box") and **Lott'd** (pronounced "Lot-dee").

First of all, say "hello" to Bocks, the "Perpetual Charity Box." Bocks welcomes within his walls all those items that have since served you and your family well. Bocks is your friend. Bocks is very low maintenance and lives in the garage. Bocks loves to receive gifts and will gladly follow you around to keep you company as you undertake these chores. You feed Bocks goodies often.

Bocks likes to share, and delivers, to individuals who have few resources, items that are useable and in good condition. From time-to-time you take the Bocks for a ride to the nearest S.O.S Shelter, Salvation Army, or any local food shelter.

Next, say "hello" to Lott'd, also known as the "List Of Things To Do." Lott'd is a very distinguished MP ("Master of all Papers"). The only list you need is Lott'd. Lott'd tracks all categories. Lott'd is an expert at keeping track of a wide variety of categories, items, errands, important things, not-so-important things, things that need to get done, picked up or dropped off, people to call, chores, reminders and places to go.

Lott'd is invaluable and dedicated. Lott'd will stay with you through thick and thin regardless of where you travel. Lott'd will become your constant companion, keeping you on track, helping you to stay the course. Lott'd may prefer to live in your datebook or calendar.

Your ability to develop good time-management habits starts with getting organized within your home. You release yourself of uncertainties and subliminal fears when you are assured your family is well prepared and cared for. When your home life is organized you will find you spend far less time looking for misplaced items and straightening unnecessary messes. You will spend less time in a constant state of worry. Less clutter, of any kind, is less stress. Less stress aids in the pursuit of better relationships among immediate family members.

Take a close look at your wardrobe. Prepare to analyze and organize. Donate to Bocks any clothing that has not been worn in a year or two (This is also tax deductible if you get a receipt for your donations). This makes it easier to organize and allows for more room to store new pieces of your wardrobe that will complete a larger combination of looks. And yes, this is the moment you must donate to Bocks all those special pieces that, as of today, are three sizes too small for you (You know exactly what I mean).

Create categories for your clothing hanging in your closet. Ask a friend whom you believe has a good sense of style to help you determine what clothing in your closet makes a professional statement. Place these garments in a section of your closet for easy access. Create a section for sport clothing, casual clothing, evening wear, etc. It also helps to create sub-categories within each section. Hanging the selection of blouses together, the array of skirts together, the slacks together and the dresses together makes it easy to choose, at a glance, the outfit you will wear for the day. Give to Lott'd a list of the simple basics you may need to purchase that will help you tie the pieces together for a variety of looks.

Think about hiring an image consultant or a personal shopper (many department stores employ those who provide this service). Organize your shoes. Create categories that coincide with your clothing. Purchase a selection of basic color heels, such as brown, black, taupe, etc., that are versatile, comfortable and professional, to mix and match with your professional outfits.

Organize your lingerie. Determine what additional type of lingerie, if any, is needed to add to your wardrobe to support a professional look. Organize your nylons. Always include in your wardrobe a selection of nylons in a variety of colors. Purchase them in pairs so that you always have an extra pair in the event of the inevitable unexpected run. Categorize, for Lott'd, clothing for your wardrobe. Cross each item off Lott'd as you make your purchases.

Until you have the time and the budget to expand your accessories, a few basics will be adequate to project a professional image. Invest in a lightweight or roller briefcase to carry your business tools. Acquire a selection of gold earrings and necklaces and silver earrings and necklaces. Wear a silver- and gold-toned watch to blend with both color groups. Organize these in a jewelry organizer. This will save you hours and help simplify jewelry-accessory choices of the day.

You will find an organized closet and well-thought-out separates and accessories not only help to improve your personal style and image, but also make dressing easier and faster, reducing the time required to coordinate daily selections and to press garments.

Consider engaging each member of the family in this process to organize his/her own wardrobes. Set free those single socks, hole-filled t-shirts, and size two shorts (from four years ago). Into Bocks go all of the clothes left by visitors during sleepovers, winter jackets that are out of style or no longer fit, shoes that have been outgrown, and sweatshirts that haven't been worn in years.

Clean out your linen and towel closets. If your oldest child is at least 12, it is probably safe to assume the crib linens go to Bocks. Mismatched, torn sheets, faded rust towels from the '60s stuffed into the back corner of the third shelf go to Bocks or a well organized, clean area/container for rags in the garage. Doilies, hankies, tablecloths ... do you use them?

Game closets, sport closets, pet cabinets, play rooms ... get Bocks ... you know the drill.

In the kitchen, organize cupboards and drawers. Throw away all of the useless disposable containers saved from prepared foods, jars, fast food containers, condiment squeeze packages, assortment of napkins, plastic utensils, old dish towels, and any other paraphernalia that simply clutter up your kitchen cupboards and drawers. Don't forget Bocks. Give to Bocks all of the kitchen gadgets you just knew you could not live without and have rarely used, such as the peel-o-matic-super-juicer-remove-the-calories-mega-vega-machine and the Snowman ice makers you bought for the kids to use during the summer months – eight years ago.

Purchase an appropriate set of stacking mixing bowls. The "odds and ends" go to Bocks. Take stock of your daily glasses, dinnerware and place settings. Do you have enough to serve dinner, even when some pieces are in the dishwasher?

How about suitable cookware? Can you prepare an entire meal at the same time with the pots, pans and skillets in your cabinets? Speaking of cooking; do you have a well-stocked condiment cabinet? An array of spice sets, salts, and condiments will save endless hours of running to the store for last-minute cooking supplies. Make a new category for Lott'd. Cross the items off Lott'd's "Kitchen" one-by-one.

Groceries are one of Lott'd's specialties. Grocery issues start in the refrigerator. Do you have three jars of mustard opened in there? Condense them down to one. Throw the other two away. Toss jars that have been in the refrigerator for at least the last six months (You may want to consider wiping with a cleaner while you're there). If you do not have the standard staples such as ketchup, mustard, mayonnaise or whatever it is your family consistently prefers, put them on Lott'd and stock up. Keep an extra jar, can, or bottle as reserve, if possible. The goal here is to make a shopping trip only once a week for the entire week's supply of food, both refrigerated and non-refrigerated.

Purchase bulk items whenever possible from buying clubs or giant discount markets. You will save money and time by purchasing in this manner items such as vegetables, fruit, tissues, frozen goods, bottled water, soft drinks, personal care supplies, vitamins, over-the-counter medications, pet supplies, laundry detergents, paper towels, trash bags, baggies, foil and cleaning supplies, to name a few.

Cleaning supplies? Note with Lott'd to clean out underneath the kitchen and bathroom sinks. Bring protection. There may be something living under there by now.

If you enjoy cooking for your family, consider preparing double portions of dinner. One dinner to eat that evening; another to freeze for a night when you may be booked elsewhere and won't have the time to prepare something else. Freezing homemade dinners is a huge time-saver, as well as a delicious and nutritious way to serve your family home-cooked meals instead of fast food while maintaining a busy work schedule. Baked turkeys and family-size hams are not only tasty, but are versatile dishes. They might possibly be a beautiful main course one evening, sandwiches for the kids the next day for lunch, and a delicious soup for the next night.

In today's market there are large selections of delicious pre-mixed, dried soups, sauces and dips. These are easy to keep fresh and can add a wonderful touch to finish dozens of simple dishes. Another fun idea your family will enjoy is to make a certain night of the week "family night out" for dinner. Make a habit to treat the entire family to a different restaurant each week, on you from your new sales-income earnings. You, the family, and Lott'd will create a restaurant category. This is not only fun, but is educational. Use it as an opportunity to introduce children to different cultures around the world.

Do you have house plants? If so, how much time do you spend watering and pruning them? Is this something you enjoy doing? Is there some one else in the household who is willing to take on that responsibility? Should you consider silks instead?

Is clutter in family rooms and bedrooms a problem? Do you find yourself experiencing embarrassing moments when unexpected guests drop in to see your house in complete disarray? The solution to what could be an enormous undertaking is simple: big empty baskets located in inconspicuous spaces in family living areas. Big basket, or "Baget," is designed for such emergencies. When the doorbell rings you rush to the family room where you quickly scoop everything off the tabletops and floor into the "Baget" and replace the lid on top. Voila! A clean room in seconds, on your way to answering the front door to greet your guests!

Do your bedrooms, especially children's rooms, have appropriate shelving for storage of books, games, prized possessions? Many children have difficulty sorting and organizing the way adults do. It is easier for them to make "sorting" projects successful if they have proper shelving, drawers, or play boxes to help them stay organized. If the storage space is appropriate, perhaps it's time to add the bedrooms to Lott'd. Bocks should be there too.

The management of a home is a big responsibility. Communication with immediate family members is vital, especially children. Family mobile phone plans are inexpensive. Sign up for one that enables your children of any age to contact you and for you to contact them at any time of any day regardless of where they are and where you or your spouse may be. If they're too young, have the adult watching them watch the phone too.

Tracking taxes, mortgages, bills, insurance, investments, legal documents and warranties, etc., is a never-ending process. This serious business deserves a space worthy of the thought and precision needed to track the security of a family. Every family needs a space, even a modest space with a desk, for home management. Computers are optional but definitely invaluable as you realize the time saved by using one in your financial planning and transfer processes while paying even normal debts. Correspondence with friends, family, and businesses is immensely simplified with e-mail. Incoming postage mail is gathered at this space, and then appropriately distributed.

Hanging files are a must to alphabetize and organize written notices, billings and important documents. These files should be organized in a way that, in the event of emergencies, another responsible adult can locate necessary information. Include identifications and pass codes to access information stored in the PC.

This office area should also be the area any member of your family can go to determine where you are located at any given time of the day and a phone number to reach you. In that space should be a list with names and numbers for emergencies, contact information, and weekly schedules for both children and adult family members. In addition to a PC or laptop, your home-management space may include a phone/fax/copy machine, a drawer with a stapler and staples, stamps, pens and pencils, paper clips, envelopes, extra hanging files, a family date book and note pad to start. Put these items on Lott'd.

Gardening, mowing, watering, weeding, fertilizing, and bedding can take much time and, for many, is a relaxing and fulfilling hobby. Invest in a gardening cart on wheels. It will store and organize pesticides, gardening tools, seeds, hoses, etc. If you delight in this activity, having all that you need at your fingertips will further enhance the experience. If you do not delight in this activity, get a gardener.

If the garage irritates you every time you walk through to get in and out of your car, or you struggle to reach the washer and dryer on laundry day, put it on Lott'd. Perhaps you can enlist the family's help and make this one a family project one weekend, finishing with a trip to the cinema afterwards for a treat. Bocks is already willing and waiting. You might as well enlist Lott'd for household improvements and repairs while you are at it.

I believe every woman who runs a household, a family, and a job, even if it is part-time, should definitely engage the services of the very minimum, a cleaning service. They are not expensive and it frees the "woman of the house" to make money that brings residual earnings (Remember the advice of Lee Iacocca). Hiring a cleaning person also eliminates spending valuable time on routine household tasks that must be repeated every week, such as cleaning toilets, mopping floors, vacuuming, scouring sinks, etc. Pay someone else to come one day a week to perform these mundane, but essential, tasks. You spend your time working on building your future. No one in your household cares who cleans the toilets — as long as they are clean!

A cleaning service one day a week for heavy cleaning will free a tremendous amount of time for you to work at other goals and spend more quality time with your family. Light cleaning will be left to you throughout the week.

Wow! So much to do. Who has time for a job? As amazing as it is, we do all of this and more. Remember, the key is to identify each area that needs improvement and get started ... even if it is oh-so-slowly. Within the year, you will have a smoother running, happier household.

Now that you've decided to take control of your future and get organized, you will need the family to pitch in, help out and support you.

Step one is family support: Call a family meeting. Introduce Bocks and Lott'd. Dress them up. Put a smile on Bocks and a flower on Lott'd. This is a big day for them and they will always want to make a good first impression. Let the family know you are going to begin to organize the house and your time. Explain to them why Bocks and Lott'd are going to be around.

Okay, you've got your family and Lott'd, Bocks, and a few other new acronym friends. For a complete listing and a much deeper discussion of this topic and chapter, check with your upline for the next scheduled "Getting Organized and Planning to Win" training at a SeneGence event. If she doesn't have a clue, call me at SeneGence headquarters.

It is now time to welcome one more friend, DB, (pronounced "Dee-Bee") your personal Date Book. In DB, record people to call, phone numbers, incidental expenses, reminders, events and every scheduled appointment.

DB has a cousin, AB, (pronounced "Abe"), your appointment book. You can find AB at beauty supply stores. AB looks like a date book but has additional columns to track the days of the week for several people. AB is wonderful tool for busy families who have children who disperse in many directions throughout the week. Rotating family chores and tracking who is doing what chore this week can be recorded in AB.

AB will help begin to teach your young children important life lessons. Taking on certain responsibilities, such as emptying the trash or picking up one's room, teaches young ones to participate in basic activities for family accountability. Successful completion of chores can be measured by placement of a stamp or star by the name of the participant for which the task was assigned. An accumulation of stars by the end of the week may be rewarded with additional privileges. What a fun way to teach children goal setting!

Lott'd, AB and your other new friends have no set boundaries. They can help with education, with entertainment, with spiritual and religious commitments and on and on. All of this work is aimed at making you more flexible, more available on a planned basis to begin building your business.

Remember, you have to "circulate to percolate." The busiest people get the most done. If you are mindful of how you spend your busy days, watching for opportunities as you encounter them, you will gather plenty of names of those who will be interested in your fabulous products on an ongoing basis as you run errands for tasks listed on Lott'd and AB.

The SeneGence *Book to Build* goes into a lot more detail than we can touch on here, so if you are a Distributor be sure to check out the Distributor "back office" at www.SeneGence.com. And if you're not a Distributor for SeneGence, well, here's one more reason why you *should* be: to get all of the tips and tricks for living an organized, efficient life that are in the full *Book to Build*.

〜 Your Turn (Chapter 21) 〜

• Refer to the Life Balance Wheel on page 208. Are you satisfied with your current outcomes within each of the life categories listed? Have you set goals for each area? If not, take the time to do so. What is not measured and attended to will simply default to an unsatisfactory outcome. Plan to live life to the fullest within each category of life. Schedule sufficient time in your date book every week to incrementally work your way towards the achievement of the goals for each category according to DSA guidelines your product purchase is refundable up to 90 percent of your last product purchase if you do not succeed in selling. Be prepared with a copy of your business plan and/or your company's compensation plan. I bet you can name three people who would be willing to help you get started.

Chapter 22
Getting Organized at Work

Managing a direct-selling business is like any other important function in your life that should be monitored and managed. You prioritize, plan and execute. Procrastination is the enemy!
— JONI

In the last chapter, we discussed getting organized in your personal life, especially at home, **Now let's talk about the business side of your new and efficient lifestyle.** It is your job to determine two things as they apply to your direct-selling business: How much profit do you want and how much time are you willing and able to apply to each of the components of The Business Balance Wheel to reach your goals?

I use my Business Balance Wheel to help Distributors (like me!) figure out how much time to spend doing what.

Determine how much profit you need to earn from your business in order to accomplish your objectives (from a new wardrobe to a new house). Then go to the Business Balance Wheel and determine what amount of time you will spend each week on various activities.

The total amount of time you devote to your business is based on your goals; Many women use 10, 20 or 40 hours a week as benchmarks. The amount of time that you spend on your business activities should directly correlate to the amount of profit, recognition and position you wish to achieve.

Imagine each component of the Business Balance Wheel (page 224, Fig. 2) as a spoke of a wheel. Looking at the business wheel, each section of the wheel has a percentage assigned to it. As you can see, a typical 40-hour workweek for the direct-selling professional would

Business Balance Wheel for Direct Sales Professionals

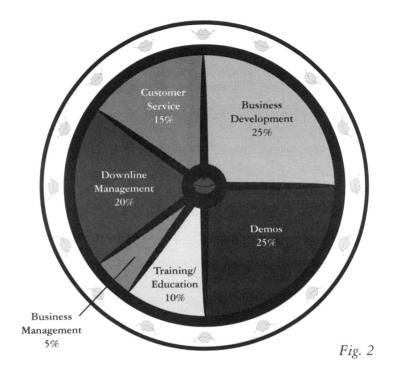

Fig. 2

ideally look something like this:

- **Business Development:** Wowing and Booking – ten hours per week
- **Generating Business:** Demonstrations – ten hours per week
- **Customer Service Management (Book to Build):** six hours per week
- **Downline Management:** eight hours per week or 1 day per week
- **Business Management:** two hours per week
- **Business Education:** four hours per week; or two days per month; or three days per quarter.

Managing a direct-selling business is like any other important function in your life that should be monitored and managed. You prioritize, plan, and execute. Procrastination is the enemy! Spending more time than you should on activities that are simple but not revenue producing will get you organized, but will not make you money!

It's important to plan each day of the week in order to be most efficient and profitable, taking advantage of each and every profit-earning opportunity possible. You must communicate this to your downline Distributors so that they may increase their earnings and profits; and you in turn increase and maximize your Downline and Group Sales Volume commission incomes as well.

So, according to the Business Balance Wheel, how are you going to spend your working time? Let's take this step by step, based on a 40-hour work week:

1. Business Development: Wowing and Booking – 25 percent or 10 hours per week.

The easiest thing to remember is this: "An empty date book is an empty pocket book." No demos on the books, no dollars in the pocket. Spend fully a quarter of your working time developing new business through wowing, then booking appointments. What is wowing and booking? Go back to Chapter 9 and read up on this essential business-building activity.

2. Business Development: Demonstration – 25 percent or 10 hours per week.

That's the goal for a "wannabe successful" Distributor: 25 percent of your business week should be spent conducting demonstrations.

It doesn't really matter whether your demos are for groups (Glamour Demos) or one-on-one (SeneBlend demos); This is your most consistent source of income from product sales and for potential commission income from sponsoring new Distributors. Ten out of every 40 working hours should be spent scheduling and conducting Glamour Demos for customers or launch demos for potential new downline Distributors.

In a study conducted by the Direct Selling Association, home demos made up 62.8 percent of the profits earned by direct sellers as a whole group. In contrast, only 3.7 percent of earnings came from "temporary location" selling such as trade shows, kiosks, or booth sales. So get used to the idea that demos are going to be at the center of your business model and business life. However, local street fairs, networking events, conferences and open houses are all great "temporary locations" at which to gather leads for future bookings.

Another important rule to remember is that to engage in 10 hours of two- to three-hour demos each week you have to schedule double that amount. In other words, if you are shooting for five two-to three-hour demos, schedule 10 because typically half of them will cancel. Life happens.

Also, remember that every Glamour Demo you conduct is also a training opportunity for one (or more) of your newer downline Distributors. You should never conduct a Glamour Demo without taking a new downline Distributor with you. Just think: Within a 40-hour workweek you know you need to spend at least eight hours training your downline. Take advantage of the hours you spend at Glamour Demos by turning them into training time for your downline as well. "On location" training is the very best way to train new Distributors.

3. Customer Service Management – 15 percent or six hours per week.

Your customer base is one of your most valuable business assets. Paying attention to your customers and following up will lead to new Distributors, reorders, up-selling, future bookings and successful product launches and volume sales and promotions. This includes placing follow-up calls within 24 to 48 hours to all new customers. Check on product performance and application techniques. Follow up to "upsell" other products that they were interested in, book possible SeneBlends demos for themselves, and so on.

Another example of customer-service activities is calling customers to remind them of special discounts and promotions as they become available. Volume discounts and sales work great when they are time-sensitive and have special meaning, e.g., associated with a holiday, time of year or a product launch. Remember our discussion in Chapter 19 about The Art of Selling?

If you want to know how successful and profitable the Art of Selling can be, talk to SeneGence Independent Distributor Melanie Forrest (Crown Princess). She ran a P.J. party promotion with a 10 percent discount on orders through her Website. She had so much traffic on her site during the promotion and sale hours that three customers couldn't even get through to place their orders. Not too bad a problem to have (though it's good to plan ahead for peak website traffic too).

Managing customer reorders and placing follow-up calls to customers when a special event like a wedding, birthday or anniversary is coming up are also good examples of good customer service.

To get the most out of customer service, you may want to re-read Chapter 18, "Customers Are Worth Their Weight in Gold."

4. Downline Management – 20 percent or eight hours per week, or one day per week.

That's right, 20 percent of your time each week should be spent on downline management. Train Distributors you have recruited to run efficient and profitable businesses early in their direct-sales careers. Why? When people are making money and building active businesses they stay excited about the career opportunity. When your downlines are excited, Distributor retention increases along with your downline commission incomes.

This includes time spent generating weekly or monthly newsletters sent to downline Distributors, along with training/meetings, conference calling, Webinars and Skype, or face-to-face meetings at your home or in a local venue.

This activity also includes scheduling time to attend Glamour Demos your downline Distributors are holding, just to provide support, encouragement and gentle direction on how to always improve.

5. Business Management: five percent or two hours per week.
This isn't a lot of your time each week, but it's an *important* time. These are those vital moments when you work on your business balance sheet, recording sales, expenses, completing sales summaries and so on. This is also the time you spend at the bank, or planning events, checking on inventory and placing orders and so on. You can see this is critical work. But be careful! Many people get lost in these activities.

Some Distributors may organize and reorganize, looking at the product on the shelves and wonder why none of it is selling. Of course time must be spent on the administrative parts of your business, but do not allow these vital activities to take you away from your revenue-producing activities. *If you find that five percent of your business week is not enough time for you to personally manage this part of your business, it's time to hire an assistant.*

6. Business Education – 10 percent or four hours per week; or two days per month; or three days per quarter.
School is never out for a professional. Plan needed time for continued education, training, inspiration, and motivation with your colleagues at company-sponsored events designed for your continued success.

Remember, the Business Balance Wheel is based on a 40-hour workweek. If you're planning to run your business on a more modest weekly time allotment, just adjust the times, not the percentages. The percentages of time spent always stay the same, whether you're working 10, 20, 30 or 40 hours a week.

Take charge of your life and forge ahead by planning to use your time wisely and steering your efforts toward balance with the Life and Business Wheels.

❧ Your Turn (Chapter 22) ❧

- Take a closer look at the Business Balance Wheel. Now use a program like Microsoft Excel or take out pen and paper and make your own balance wheel for Business. Print your balance wheel out. Now track your time over the next couple of weeks and see how your actual business compares to the ideal balance you visualized in your balance wheel. Do you need to revise your balance wheel? Or do you need to revise how you are spending your time? Only you can answer these questions.

- Before you go too far with finding the right balance in your business, make sure you have answered this question: *"What do I really want in life?"* If you're not sure, go back now and reread Chapter 8: What Do You Really Want?

- If you had eight additional hours a week, how would you spend them? Write your answer down and be specific. Now reread the preceding chapter and see if there are any opportunities for you to find eight additional hours in your week. Look closely at your balance wheels. Are they in balance?

Part Three:
Visions

Chapter 23
SeneSisters are Amazing Entrepreneurs

The sisterhood that Joni and SeneGence breed is amazing. We are all truly SeneSisters, no matter whose downline we are in. We are always here for each other, for Joni and our company, with love, compassion, passion, empathy, understanding and encouragement. We have each other's backs at all times, coaching and encouraging every step of our journey; not only in our SeneGence careers, but we are here to carry each other in our life's journeys as well.

— PAMELA BENNETT, SeneGence Independent Distributor (Lady) and Florida State Leader

One very unique thing about SeneGence in our industry is the precious sisterhood of women who embody the values and opportunity of this company.

They have received the gift of this business graciously, its products and its opportunity, and are working hard to pass the gift along to all the women they in turn meet.

We share a culture that capitalizes on relationships among women who have mutual respect for one another. Each SeneGence Independent Distributor brings certain talents, beauty and skills to the business and some of these women continue to develop and refine the notion of what the business really is and ought to look like. We call these women "SeneSisters."

It's an exclusive club that is inclusive too: Every SeneGence Independent Distributor is welcome as a SeneSister. You demonstrate your membership in the "sisterhood" by building your business, sponsoring others and participating in company events; by becoming an important member of the whole.

SeneSisters are very entrepreneurial and individualistic. Each of us has her own style in business and in life. Over the years we have grown to love and to appreciate each other.

SeneSisters are also highly adventurous. Every one was, at one time or another, willing to jump in and become part of an effort to build an organization from the ground up. Together we have created this company and this culture of SeneSisters.

There's no space and time within the culture of SeneSisters. When we talk among ourselves it's as if we left off minutes ago, even when we haven't spoken for months.

And we're very careful to support one another; edify and physically help one another in any way that we can. We expand this loving care to their families as well.

Every SeneGence Independent Distributor is amazing. But these women we call "SeneSisters" were physically and mentally prepared to teach a massive new customer base about products that had never been seen and taught before. You have to be strong willed and determined to be able to do that.

So when I meet a new SeneGence Independent Distributor, I am already awed by that person and I don't even know her yet. I am awed because she is willing to insert herself into her community and teach women a whole new approach to making skin more beautiful with our innovative technologies in color and skin care.

It takes a lot to win the respect of this group, but it's not complicated: You earn the respect of the Sisterhood of SeneSisters by showing up and "doing it" – by being a builder; being someone who can become a part of a mastermind group. You earn respect by being someone who helps to resolve challenges or problems, by consistent sponsoring, by consistent selling, and by showing up and participating at company events.

A good example of "showing up" is SeneGence Independent Distributor Leta Greene. Leta has been with us since our second year of business, but I didn't get to know her until her ninth year because she has been actively selling, moving from one state to the next, raising children, as well as taking care of her husband after his heart attack and after he was by hit by a bus. There's no question she's a SeneSister. During her young family's growth years she was simply unable to attend company events, but was immediately recognized as a member of the Sisterhood as soon as she did appear. She's been very present and her contributions have been felt by all; just not seen until lately as her life has allowed.

When I was a single mother, my son Alan woke up one morning and we remembered that he had a karate tournament to get to. Alan said, "Mom I don't want to go."

I said, "Honey don't you have teammates who are depending on you? You must keep your commitment to your teammates and go."

So, he dressed for the event, but wasn't happy about going.

I sat in the bleachers watching the event and watching him compete. The participants began moving into breakout matches and next thing I knew, Alan won the tournament! It was a clear lesson to Alan that showing up is 80 percent of winning!

Consistently showing up is also what counts in becoming a SeneSister.

It is difficult to support people to succeed when they don't show up in one way or another. If you want to compete, if you want a shot at winning the tournament, you have to show up first. "Showing up" starts with demo-ing and sponsoring. That's what SeneSisters do.

SeneSister-hood is an elite group – they're the 20 percent of the group who really make things happen for themselves and for the company.

I'd like to mention a few of these remarkable women. Each has taught me beautiful lessons along the way and won my admiration and heart for giving her unique gifts to our cause.

First on that list would have to be SeneGence Queen Jeri Taylor-Swade, our Washington State Founder and first Nevada State Leader. Her unequalled success is a reflection of her amazing gifts and talents. Jeri has been with us from the very beginning of SeneGence. Through periods of growth and periods of challenge, she has strived to make sound business decisions and judgments. Jeri is smart and outgoing, but she is consistently focused on building her business and behaving like a professional. Her level-headedness has gained her love and respect from Distributors throughout the company and across many continents. Jeri has played many roles in her life. She's a hard worker and a team player. Jeri worked to put her husband through medical school; she is a contributing citizen to her community and has appeared in plays, coached cheerleading squads, and is a political activist. Jeri also plays a prominent role in the Direct Selling Women's Alliance, an organization for women in direct sales. She coauthored a book on direct sales and was featured in award-winning DVDs on the industry and presented as a "master" in a CD training series for others who have chosen careers in direct sales.

From SeneGence Crown Princess and California State Leader Sheila Young I have learned graciousness. Sheila is the epitome of that quality. Underneath that, she's a bling-loving go-getter who really knows how to be a businesswoman as she became an entrepreneur with husband Mike immediately following graduation from high school. But there is always this overarching graciousness, and a pure angelic quality, to everything she does. Sheila is an inspiring, sweet leader to thousands.

Lauren Syverud is the youngest woman to have earned the title of SeneGence Crown Princess. She became a Crown Princess, responsible for at least $1 million in annual sales at the age of 28, and is one who is able to accomplish anything she puts her mind to. She looks to me like an angel (in fact, we pictured her as an angel in a SeneGence ad). Now a young mother of two active children, Lauren is an articulate company spokesperson and beauty expert, and is a fantastic trainer.

I have learned a higher level of spirituality, and the full meaning of motherhood, by being with SeneGence Royal and Utah State Leader Leta Greene. Just having the privilege of eating with her, in her home with her family, I have learned to treasure more my role as a mother and wife. She is an intelligent, directed, animated, outspoken individual and a shining example of how to balance a family with a business. Leta is a giving mentor and leader to her downline and to women members of her church.

As I have said elsewhere in this book, I don't let others easily alter my perceptions of reality. These SeneSisters influence me with their personal qualities; gifts that shine above the norm.

I'm inspired by SeneGence Lady and Florida State Leader Pamela Bennett's natural energy and stunning beauty, surpassed only by her charismatic personality. Among other things, Pamela is an under-the-sea diver and a ballroom dancer. Her mere presence inspires us to exercise and stay healthy. I have seen people awed by her beauty, impressed with her knowledge, entertained by her personality and led by her instruction. Her passion, people skills and drive make her a natural leader.

I am grateful to Lady Karole Lewis, for her steady mind and common-sense ability to communicate to others our company practices and product knowledge. She is a leader among leaders, always teaching and guiding others to improve. Karole came to SeneGence as a businesswoman traveling around the world, and was working in downtown Manhattan when the September 11 attacks led her into trying something new. She found us, and has been an inspired leader in our organization ever since. She is also an accomplished opera singer, performing at Lincoln Center in New York. Karole is an amazingly well-balanced woman who lives what we teach, and shows we can indeed have it all!

Royal Katie Sevenants is an amazingly consistent performer, even though she is the mother of three very active girls and is devoted to them full time. Katie, incidentally, has in her front yard the most beautiful tree I have ever seen. What a fitting symbol for this beautiful woman. We love Katie, her kids, her pets and her tree. She is an example of balancing life – from participating in women's groups and as an activity leader for her girls' many activities throughout the year, to a growing a downline and running a business. She's a wonderful role model and citizen of her community. As our Washington State Leader,

Katie shows us there is always a way to "get it done."

SeneGence Royal and Oklahoma State Leader Dawn Christian is a wonder to watch as she balances a full-time career with home life and a growing SeneGence business. She joined SeneGence as the mother of three young children under five years old. She has over the years been able to carve out more time for her SeneGence business while running her boutique and maintaining a balance and focus on her home life. Dawn has grown from lacking self confidence when I first met her to a women who knows what she wants and knows how to get the job done. She committed herself to choose to walk the path of personal growth and did the work needed to internalize strength and confidence. Through the years it's been a pleasure to watch Dawn discover how to articulate exactly what she wants to achieve and determine a course to do so. Dawn is a "doer," inspiring others through her own actions to expect more of themselves, while building a legacy of success for her children.

SeneGence Lady and Georgia State Leader Bridget Lambros is yet another SeneSister who seems to be able to do it all. She's led a large downline organization while performing the duties of a minister's wife. She has raised her children, sending them to college and, eventually, marriage while building her SeneGence career over the years.

SeneGence Royal and California State Leader Kelly Robertson is a natural-born leader with an attitude that is positively infectious. She expects nothing but the best from herself, her daughters, and others. Kelly is a pleasure to spend any amount of time with as she encourages and motivates with every word that she speaks. Her experience working for the U.S. Army, helping families of fallen soldiers, has helped to prepare her for a leadership role in helping others to succeed and offering needed support while doing so. She committed to not only learn the business of direct sales but to also learn the trade of beauty by becoming a certified makeup artist. Although a makeup artistry certification is not necessary to have as a successful SeneGence Distributor, Kelly wanted to ensure she had the correct understanding of a broad range of cosmetic applications to pass on to her downline Distributors and customers. Kelly is the perfect example of how leaders lead others to success through example.

Royal and Nevada State Leader Cathy Hoolihan is simply a joy to be with. She is known to me for her honesty and forthrightness, which I admire immensely. She is a powerful woman who is organized; a builder, all-the-while caring for her family. Cathy loves people and people love her. In fact, if there's a party, Cathy is at the center of it ... and more people are there because they get to spend time with Cathy.

When I was on the road most of the time back in 2005 and 2006, training the sales force to develop as home and office demo-ing direct-sales professionals, SeneGence Royal and Arizona State Leader Cathy Rice appeared in the audience at many events. First in one state and then another and another. Little did I know that her other job as a flight attendant made that possible. I noticed her sitting in the crowd in city after city and at first didn't know who she was, but then made it a priority to meet her. She would appear at various locations with new Distributors in tow, listening, building, learning and transforming from a trade-show oriented Distributor to one who really understood the direct-sales opportunity of home and officer demo-ing in "her own back yard." What a role model! Cathy unselfishly supports and nurtures SeneGence Distributors to succeed across the borders of many states.

SeneSister Distributor Kristin Zumwalt is my dearest friend from childhood. Up to this point Kristin has been a SeneGence Distributor to purchase products for herself and her immediate family. I love her so much. She and her family changed my life through their role modeling and endless loving kindness. Her consistent friendship and support have carried me through rough waters as well as brought joy to my days in good times too. Thank you for being there with and for me, Kristin.

Distributor Judy Gaunt is also among this top tier of SeneGence women introducing the product to thousand of women in search of products that really work. Judy played the leading role in introducing products of

SeneGence to the Northwest U.S. coast. I would drop anything to help her. Thank you, Judy.

Royal and Texas State Leader Kaylen Young is a ball of energy, a real "spitfire" (lovingly said). Kaylen is an efficient trainer and teacher for glamour and color cosmetics, and has taught the entire sales force great tips and tricks of the trade on many occasions. I thank you for inspiring so many of our talented and aspiring SeneBlends Make Up Artists during various company events.

Maiden and Wisconsin State Leader Deb Sell is a prime example of how to build a customer base and a downline of SeneGence Distributors in one area of the country and then build both again after having moved her family from one state to another. A retired school teacher, Deb is a thorough and inspirational trainer. Thank you for sharing your talents, Deb.

Royal and Australian Leader of Distributor Development Mary Ann Pinto – all I have to say is "Wow!" You are a woman after my own heart. Thank you for being the leader of SeneGence for the entire outback continent. You are a first-class entrepreneur and we are privileged to have your allegiances, my dear. Thank you.

Finally, Distributor Priscilla Markham, you've helped to make this journey fun. Thank you for your friendship, hospitality, and for making me laugh as we journey down this road together.

There are others, too, whom I could easily add to this list. Some are (or were) temporarily SeneGence leaders at one time or another throughout the years and played a role in the growth of SeneGence for a period of time. I send my heartfelt thanks to these women for the contributions they made. Though they are not mentioned specifically in this accounting, they have been an essential part of what SeneGence has become and achieved today. I believe they were delivered to us by God to make the contribution they were sent to make before moving on to other endeavors. May your paths be blessed.

Thank you one and all for your contributions, making SeneGence and the SeneSisterhood possible.

Your Turn (Chapter 23)

- Reread the brief stories of some of the SeneSister leaders in the preceding chapter. Does one or more of these stories sound like yours? Or like the woman you want to be? If you haven't joined us already, why not go to www.senegence.com right now and find a distributor near you to help you get started? (Okay ... that's an outright sponsoring plug ... and I am proud to admit it!)

Chapter 24
The Future of Direct Sales

Joni Rogers-Kante is an exceptional teacher. When you train with her, you can actually see a light around her. We all hope that light will continue to shine well into the future of this company.

— LAUREN SYVERUD, SeneGence Independent Distributor (Crown Princess)

There are plenty of pundits and professors who say direct selling is the sales channel for the future. I agree.

Direct-selling companies, including SeneGence International, cover a broad range of products and services, from animal and pet care products to wine collections. Cosmetics, clothing, pots and pans, legal services, phone services, insurance ... these are just a few of the many categories in which direct selling companies are engaged throughout the world.

If you're looking for an industry segment that will keep growing despite the roller-coaster world economy, I think direct selling is the place. In the United States alone, direct selling accounts for about $30 billion each year in sales. And those sales are expected to continue growing in the future, according to the Direct Selling Association.

It's important to remember that more than 70 percent of those sales take place in somebody's home. People crave the company of other people, and technology doesn't change that. As social networking media such as Facebook, Twitter and phone texting become ever more important in our society, the opportunities for face-to-face contact and direct selling will only continue to increase, along with the tools that keep people in touch with each other.

I like to think that the direct selling industry is a powerful, positive force in our world. Direct sales companies continue to offer anyone who is willing to get off her laurels the opportunity to build substantial income and security with virtually no huge upfront investment. I started this company with no money other than what I reinvested through earnings. You can too. Where else can you find opportunities like this?

The only thing that can impede this industry's natural growth is government interference; laws that inhibit independent contractors who are business owners. This is a global concern and many governments make it difficult for independent contractors to prosper, both in the United States and elsewhere.

Millions upon millions of dollars gathered from direct sales are donated to charities that help support causes around the world. We are a generous clan of people who help others. These causes range from supporting impoverished communities and nations to helping animals and rainforests, reducing global warming and much more. SeneGence itself has a sister non-profit company called the "MakeSense Foundation," that supports women and children in need.

The Make Sense Foundation exists because we SeneGence Distributors fund it as we prosper. Portions of our Distributor Application Fee and product sales are transferred to the Foundation. We hold annual fund raisers and donate a good portion of the earnings from specific sales tools to this cause and use the funds to support organizations that are committed to helping women and children who need help. I've been there ... how about you?

The opportunities for direct sellers are boundless and, as I have said, technology is only increasing the opportunities for direct-selling professionals. If you have the willingness and a desire to succeed, the world awaits you.

You and I could probably name a handful of companies that sell only on the Web. But mostly those are impersonal product lines and aren't comparable to sales of highly personal products such as cosmetics and in particular SeneCeuticals (a higher grade "cosmeceutical" because ours really works!).

Personal care and color cosmetics will remain a very visible product category in direct selling, as it is a highly consumable reorder product category of goods. The most effective direct-selling companies and distributors will make ample use of new technologies to "reach out and touch" others around the world while also capitalizing on the personal nature of our business.

So to our younger Distributors – Gen X or Gen Y or Millennials, and whatever comes after, I strongly encourage all of you to embrace an independent Distributor lifestyle early in life. Your business will continue to grow as you do, and your high comfort with new technologies will enable you to build customer loyalty while providing excellent customer service at a higher level than was possible with the generations who came before you.

The point is that "smart" phones, iPads, laptops and other personal mobile devices, as well as social-networking tools such as Facebook and Twitter, can be put to good use by the direct-sales professional who understands how to include them in her customer contact routine and Distributor training process. These tools can bring you closer to customers and downline Distributors, not further away. They create opportunities to maintain regular contact with both between scheduled demos, company live events, and so on. It means we get to meet more people and see them more often than we used to. It also means we need to keep our "face on" as we never know who will call on Skype or similar programs any time of the day or evening!

Modern communications are also having a dramatic effect on the supply-chain side of our business at SeneGence, and probably at every other manufacturing business. For instance, when our company was recently looking for a specific set of new manufacturing and training capabilities for one of our product lines, we did a little research and guess where the top manufacturing trainers were located? India. So, that's where you go to learn about that particular issue. Make an appointment, schedule the dates online, book a flight and hotel, all in the matter of minutes, and all in a days work. It's not too tough or too expensive to book a ticket to India, jump on a plane and take classes at the facility. Getting on a flight to somewhere around the world today is easier than booking a ticket on a cross-country bus trip to another city of yesteryear. That's exactly what more and more of us will be doing, taking advantage of a global community and eliminating barriers to learning and expanding. The world indeed is our oyster.

Meanwhile there is also a growing demand for local contacts and continuity of relationships in our own local communities. If I know somebody who can get to me what I need and we've already done business together, I'm going to seek that person in most cases, whether it be face-to-face or via the Web. That fact hasn't changed for me personally or for consumer confidence.

Technology is also enabling us to reach out in a more personal way to Distributors and customers in distant cities. We conduct SeneGence trainings via the web on each Tuesday and Thursday of every week from our International Offices here in Southern California, And we broadcast monthly training sessions live to groups of new Distributors who have gathered together in various cities in the countries where SeneGence Distributors live. We can see each other on our computer screens, and so we visually connect as we share ideas and tips.

Here's how it looks: We typically start off the training sessions on Friday morning. I bake quiche at home and ship it to each location where there are groups of our Distributors gathered, so they can join us for the morning meeting and breakfast just like they were here with us. We eat the same meals. They work in real time from the same workbooks. And they hear every word and ask questions as they are encountered.

Lunch and dinner are catered for the group here in Southern California. Remote locations arrange a potluck. We train, eat, and work simultaneously — around the world.

In past years, these same Distributors would have to fly in from around the globe to participate in these trainings. They had to book hotel rooms and we had to have production people producing the meetings, event planners arranging transportation, and so on. So the cost of doing business for these trainings has been greatly reduced, both for the company and for the Distributors.

The Internet has, at SeneGence as elsewhere, become a standard tool for the retail customer to order products. Any responsible business owner should build a way for customers to access and to pay for the company products 24 hours a day, seven days a week. In fact, when a potential customer calls into the corporate office or sends an e-mail to find a Distributor, we only recommend those who are using our online Web-based tools, as we believe those Distributors are in business to stay in business.

One area that continues to develop for direct sellers is the international opportunity. In our company, a distributor can choose to deal locally, building a residual income from the growth of downline distributors, or broadly, including building downlines in other countries where SeneGence operates. In SeneGence you may build a downline organization and receive commission income for doing so in any country in which SeneGence operates. That's a huge earning opportunity for one who likes to travel or not.

I remind myself that there are more than 450 ports of call throughout the world, each one representing the opportunity to engage in trade, each with storage facilities, ship docks, airports and so on. That translates into women from all walks of life looking for products that really work. If you aspire to be a dominating product branch and company in the direct-selling industry, the question is why limit the company or its distributors to only one market? Not us! The world awaits!

I named the company "SeneGence International" from the onset. SeneGence began its global life with our markets in Canada and Australia, and we are committed to continue the process of expanding our international business – and yours.

As I have said throughout this book, you create a picture in your mind and in your heart of what you want your business to look like. And you have to work at it, every single day, for 10 or 20 years if that's what it takes – but have fun and make great friends along the way. I have no doubt that we will soon be in 100 or more countries. This gift that we and now you have will expand around the world and touch the lives of millions. (Hmmmmmm ... where did I hear that before?).

We, as a group of women that includes all women of the world in our sisterhood, are building a company that will expand and grow and affect directly and indirectly the lives of millions of women now and in future generations.

The concept of Million Dollar Lips has come a long way since this company started. We have spread the gospel of women working together for a common benefit into many countries and now hundreds of thousands of households. We are still at the beginning stages, having only just completed most of the product line and Distributor-support tools and programs. I hope you will be encouraged, better yet excited, to join us on this amazing journey.

Above all, I hope you will come to see how you too can choose to live life in love and abundance as a result of some of the ideas I have tried to present in this book. If you have, consider it my gift to you; a gift that was given to me by God and by other benefactors in my life that I now pass along freely.

May you also pass this gift along to other women you know or will eventually meet along your journey. We have choices in life, and we have the opportunity before us to live our lives as women with freedom, independence and strength. By sharing this message, you become a member of a SeneSisterhood that is spreading widely and bringing hope to our children and sisters in need.

Remember, above all, to choose to live life in love and abundance. And be willing to work for it. You can do it!

Love,
Joni